INSPIRATION

OP

3<u>50</u>

D1558227

POWER THINKING

POWER THINKING

Everyman's Highway to Healing and Creative Thinking

by
BROTHER MANDUS

Published by
ARTHUR JAMES LIMITED
THE DRIFT, EVESHAM, WORCS.

First Edition 1966
First Paperback Edition 1980
© Brother Mandus 1966

ISBN 0 85308 224 7

ACKNOWLEDGMENT

The poems in this book have been generously con-
tributed by my good and loyal friend, "Mac", of
The Sanctuary, 476 Lytham Road, Blackpool, Lancs.

Made and printed in Great Britain by
Purnell & Sons Ltd, Paulton (Bristol) and London

DEDICATION

This book is humbly dedicated by the author to *Every* man and *Every* woman, their sons and daughters, knowing that their wondrous powers of mind and personality, when recognised and released, will promote their health, happiness, and highest creative achievement.

CONTENTS

THY WILL BE DONE

Thy kingdom come. Thy will be done in earth, as it is in heaven.—MATTHEW 6: 10 (The Lord's Prayer).

Thy Will be done . . . We sit and sigh
With folded hands and tear-dimmed eye;
Beset with ills we crave no cure,
Only the patience to endure.
"It is His Will." Then must we be
Content with grey-gowned poverty,
Down barren years to plod our way
From cloudy night to dreary day?

* * *

God's Will for you, God's Will for me,
In constant perpetuity,
Is beauty, harmony and love
On earth below, in realms above.
Healing of body, mind and soul:
A balanced, poised and perfect whole.
The children of a King are we—
Joyous, invincible and free.

Thy Will be done . . . Lo! from the ground
Spring countless miracles profound.
On every bush a jewel glows,
The dewdrop and the damask rose.

9

Thy Will be done . . . Fling wide Heaven's bars
To make a pathway for the stars,
Venus and Jupiter proclaim
The matchless glory of His Name.

Thy Will be done, Thy wondrous Plan
Alike for angel and for man.
Stand forth and know yourselves to be
Co-heirs of His Divinity.
Immaculate and unafraid,
In His Almighty image made.
The Father, from His peerless throne
Bestows Perfection on His own.

"MAC"

Chapter 1

YOUR HIGH DESTINY

THROUGHOUT THE YEARS of man's awakening consciousness he has striven to understand the mystery of life and the mind in which he experiences personality and achievement.

Philosophers have led us into profound and often complicated concepts of man and the universe. Mystics have shared their vision of the spiritual nature of creation, and every religion postulates patterns of thought and action designed to ensure the well-being of the individual and the community.

The psychologist studies human behaviour, observes inner compulsions and seeks to understand the mystery of intellect and the complexities of personality. He works to heal mental disturbances and to develop methods of establishing positive and harmonious expression.

Many books have been written proclaiming every discovery about the mind of man and his outreach. Millions of words have described and taught the power of positive thinking through cultivating and controlling every aspect of thought, memory, imagination, will-power and emotion. Inevitably, much of this teaching has embraced the spiritual principles of love, faith and prayer.

As I survey all that so many talented people have written about this central miracle of mind and personality I have only one deep conviction to share with you; and that revolves round an urgent need for an all-embracing and all-pervading simplicity in every approach to the study of the mind and of man's infinite potential evolution.

In so complex a subject there are simple principles which are often overlooked. We are endowed with faculties whereby every man, woman and child can embark on wondrous adventures of positive thinking and magnificent creative experience.

But, as individuals and nations, we are in grave danger of missing our real goal of peace, happiness, health and progressive prosperity. As our mental powers become increasingly effective we grow more self-reliant and tend to reduce our dependence on the spiritual aspects of our nature. Knowledge without wisdom is a catastrophe. Life without love is destruction.

We are all involved in the greatest intellectual expansion the world has ever known. Knowledge about every aspect of life and creation is multiplying at remarkable speed. The total knowledge gained through many thousands of decades has more than doubled in volume in the last hundred years. *And every twenty years from now on it will double again!* No wonder man begins to see himself as the supreme arbiter of his environment and destiny!

Make no mistake about it, knowledge is power—for good or ill, according to our use of it!

Throughout the human scene we see this exultant and feverish pursuit of intellectual stature and corresponding works. In our educational system and through the sciences, industry, business, the professions and government we behold the overwhelming emphasis on the creative power of mind through knowledge to produce outstanding achievements. Yet we also see the multiplying problems pervading the lives of individuals and nations. There are more stresses and strains than ever before. Despite great knowledge and skill in the medical profession, mental breakdowns increase and much physical sickness prevails, as statistics show us each year.

Alongside the amazing productivity and rising standards of living which our quickened intellects project, as a world society we have become the most proficient killers of our own kind. In our lifetime we have exterminated close to one hundred million men, women and children, to say nothing of the vast destruction of cities and their traditions.

Knowledge has become very precious, but life very cheap. In the midst of so much that is exciting and good, something is disastrously wrong with our outlook and mental attitudes; something so vital that, unless it is sublimated and healed, the multiplying powers we deploy as a world family will simply end in world suicide and the loss of our culture for perhaps hundreds of years.

One of the most significant pointers to the challenge facing everyone is the expanding world population. Without going into a mass of figures and detail the present trends of increase will double it within the next thirty-five years. If we find it difficult to live harmoniously with three thousand million people now, it is easy to imagine the multiplied problems of relationships with six thousand millions.

These world pressures, intensified by growing educational standards in a massive eastern population, the demands for living space, food, water and a thousand related necessities, will stretch and challenge every aspect of man's intellect, technology and wisdom

Beyond every problem and achievement the question of personal relationships is vital to survival as a race. It is no longer something to relegate haphazardly to some distant future. The emergency stands stark and clear before every living soul here and now.

All this is, of course, well-known to everyone. From government right through the social structure, our leaders, teachers, ministers and people seek the right answers. But we are in a trap, struggling to escape from a cage of our own making; and until we see the only real truth, and have the courage to open the only door, we shall continue the imprisonment and restriction we have unwittingly inflicted on ourselves.

Our civilisation has unfolded through the expansion of intellect, the resultant accumulation of knowledge and the creative use of it. With the unique technical intensity of western nations the development of machines and electronics has revolutionised productivity. It is the most astonishing revelation of the power of man's mind that the world has ever known.

With the ever-quickening advance of technology we begin to realise that machines can be devised to accomplish almost every task which hitherto required human labour and attention. We are, indeed, entering an age when computers, automation and mechanical techniques will one day largely eliminate or reduce the need for people to work. So far we have managed, more or less, to keep labour employed in this multiplying economy, but signs are visible of the shape of things to come. As machines take on more and more control and production, so ultimately will less man-power be required.

To compensate, we see already the move to reduce working hours for the same pay. This problem is rapidly intensifying in the United States and Europe and must spread everywhere. Recently, for example, a British factory, with expensive machinery, began the experiment of a three-day working week for full pay, devised in shifts so that the machines could produce twenty-four hours a day.

Whatever approach is made, it is obvious that the entire economic structure of the West would collapse if the majority of people became unemployed without money to buy the products which machines create. This new kind of problem will inevitably become acute in the future because it demands an entirely new outlook not only by governments and spiritual leaders but also by each one of us.

With good cause we have a traditional and spiritual belief that man must work. He must be creatively occupied in order to maintain health, happiness and to fulfil his nature in achievement. Yet countless people from the next generation onwards may well be paid *not* to work in the economic structure; and countless others may be required to work only very limited hours.

This will involve a complete change of long-held beliefs which must be replaced by new and creatively satisfying activities. Perhaps one of the greatest challenges to successful human evolution may depend on how we solve this new factor of increasing leisure. A civilisation could well die of inertia, or erupt in dangerous ways, if machines were to rule man and eliminate his inner yearning for the full use of his faculties in service.

The real problem facing all humanity is one of relationship. All stress, conflict, breakdowns, wars, personal unhappiness and a high percentage of sickness stem from negative patterns of behaviour.

Great forces are exerted through every community to solve these human problems by intellectual methods of expediency; but they tend to ignore the spiritual laws which govern every aspect of human well-being, and progress is limited accordingly.

The voices which call and whisper in the wilderness—warning, guiding, pleading—are drowned in the confusion of man, the so-called supreme thinker. Spiritual truths are relegated, more often than not, to a very inferior position in the daily affairs of state and business.

We are now so accustomed to watch the involved interplay of political parties, great business combines, the armed forces, and the social scene that the mere *individual* —no matter how illumined—feels helpless and inadequate when thinking of a way to change it.

In this we see our weakest point in the world scene. As the collective opinion and power of society increases, the individual sense of responsibility and effectiveness likewise decreases. Yet it is a simple fact that in the final analysis each person is the only real power in the community. The nation, or the world family, represents the expression of *every* individual who lives in it. The mind of every living soul is thus linked with every other mind, and directly affects, for good or ill, the total attitudes, expression and experience of the whole.

The world's most urgent need now is for the re-focusing of attention on the "life-power" of the individual; we should develop mental capacities, and balance them with a new vision of spiritual truth. Unless the intellectual faculties of each individual are guided by the almighty creative powers of love, faith and wisdom, he is like the captain of a ship trying to sail the oceans without engine or compass.

In the midst of war Sir Winston Churchill said, "Never in the field of human conflict was so much owed by so many to so few." It is a truth that never before was so great a responsibility laid upon each man, woman and child as today—a responsibility to make a personal breakthrough and provide a constructive contribution to universal safety, sanity and evolution. The well-being of future generations may well depend on how quickly, one by one, the people of this generation awaken to this sense of high destiny by accepting personal responsibility for cultivating their spiritual-mental powers and expressing them in every relationship.

We must, urgently, begin to tackle world problems by concentrating on our own personalities and the way we express them. In so doing we shall not only promote our own immediate well-being but also directly influence for good the people around us, at home, at work, and throughout the nation and world community. To realise this is the only true and lasting contribution we can make to the security of our own families and the family of mankind.

It is worthy of our greatest, concentrated attention. Certain it is that the only asset we possess is our life, and the only assets of a nation are the lives of every one in it. Though we gain every material objective and lose our own soul we are lost indeed—as individuals. It is the same with a nation or the world. Man cannot live by bread alone.

That is why I seek, lovingly and humbly, to share the thoughts in this book with YOU—the individual, my friend, my brother or sister.

Let us break free from every kind of limitation, fixed idea or custom. Then I know we will be able to share the gardens of our minds together and, quite simply, pause to behold what fruits we can harvest. In this, let us be two simple people intent only on helping each other to clear a jungle of weeds so that we may create the fruits and flowers we seek.

We are, therefore, not so concerned here with the mighty thoughts and concepts of great thinkers. We want to know only those truths that apply to everyone; to the rich or poor, to the highly educated or to a girl in an African village. Let us search for powers we can understand which can be released into immediate creative good. Let us accept that everyone involved in this miracle of life possesses gifts equal to our own in a thousand ways of potential expression. And let us realise that what we discover together is equally true for all.

In the next chapter we shall begin at the beginning, and concentrate on the real YOU and YOUR MIND.

POWER THOUGHTS

1 The quickening evolution of knowledge and intellectual ability intensifies the complexity of the political, scientific, economic, social and individual way of life.

2 It both challenges and invites a deeper concentration on the importance of every man, woman and child as integral parts of the world pattern.

3 Beyond intellectual achievement is the vital need for a new scientific recognition of spiritual principles which are central to harmonious relationships between people.

4 You, the individual, possess powers which are capable of infinite extension to promote your happiness and health and the successful fulfilment of all objectives which are true to your nature.

THE CHOSEN

Ye have not chosen me, but I have chosen you, and ordained
you, that ye should go and bring forth fruit, and that your
fruit should remain; that whatsoever ye shall ask of the
Father in my name, he may give it you.—JOHN 15: 16.

"Ye have not chosen Me." Amidst earth's glamour
He steals unsought, unheeded, to your side.
Deaf to His voice above the ceaseless clamour,
You hearken to the blandishments of pride.

"Ye have not chosen Me." Your life's oblation
Squandered to pay the price of fleeting fame;
Blind to the vision of your dedication
Will you not turn and follow whence He came?

"But I have chosen you." Down through the ages
They left their nets and from their kinsmen sped;
Wise with a wisdom mightier than the sages,
They took the upward pathway where He led.

Yet once again He comes, the Disregarded,
Bidding you spurn the pomps of mortal day;
The tawdry triumphs of the world discarded,
To tread a blest and consecrated way.

*   *   *

" Ye have not chosen Me." With tireless yearning
Throughout the years I call My servants true.
Now, with Divine Illumination burning,
Thankfully know that I have chosen you.
"MAC"

Chapter 2

YOUR WONDER-WORKING MIND

EVER SINCE MAN became aware of self-existence and his ability to think and, therefore, to create personality and experience, he has sought to understand the mysteries of his mind and how it functions. This we have established.

We now leap from earth to the stars. Basically we leap from matter into the invisible yet all-powerful reaches of the mind. We move in the midst of the Laws of Consciousness through which man creates, and we increasingly become aware of the Laws which govern and mould the universe, the world and all it contains.

Since all intensive research leads to profound thinking and concepts, so much specialised knowledge is often too complicated for the layman to understand or implement in his own experience. And, moreover, the vastness of the literature expressing the findings and techniques of the researchers makes it very difficult for the ordinary man or woman to absorb it all.

My purpose is, therefore, not to write as a specialist, but rather to come to you as a friend and to talk to you, very simply, about the wonderful gifts we all possess in this mind of ours in which we have our being. This will lead you to accept and implement one simple and basic Law which can transform all your thinking, harmonise every mental-emotional attitude, and produce a constant flow of multiplying good on every level of experience.

The relaxed and ideal setting for this would be in your own home. As I write I can imagine a warm fireside, two cosy armchairs, a cup of tea, and you and I freely chatting about these little-understood but exciting facts, our problems and our way of life. There are so many fascinating lessons to learn from past experience and from our present situation. And, of course, we are both vitally interested in what we may expect to come about in the future.

In this day and age when we know so much, the extraordinary truth is that we know so little about man himself! So let us begin with this mysterious being—YOU.

Who are you? Where did you come from? Whither are you going? Three simple questions—but nobody can give us comprehensive and complete answers! We can, however, recognise and understand some vital aspects of the truth. It is most refreshing and encouraging to stand away from ourselves, from the habitual ruts into which we all fall, and look at ourselves with clearer vision.

Who are you? Well—you accept, of course, your own sharp sense of identity. From childhood until now you have developed your character and personality through your many experiences. You have a vivid memory of the main events in your life, some of which brought you great joy and others which were intensely sad. You have achieved great success in some things and devastating failure in others. Some of your relationships with other people, in your home or at work, have produced abiding peace and happiness. And, no doubt, other associations will have been fraught with pain, frustration, anxiety and perhaps even tragedy.

You have accumulated considerable knowledge about most of the things which interested you. Your way of life is now like a pavement you have laid down from the beginning, leading to the position in which you now find yourself.

You have always been intensely aware of your body. And it is true that a vast amount of your experience has come to you through the constant use of your physical senses. You enjoy most things in life through your ability to contact experience through your unique brain, eyes, ears, heart, bones, nerves, arms, legs, stomach, flesh and blood.

What an amazing machine is your body! And how little we have to do to maintain or motivate it! We command it to walk and, somehow, it walks; we lift an arm or move our fingers, write a letter or read a book; when our eyes focus on any outward scene it comes alive and we recognise and appreciate its form and beauty. Food tastes good, and we enjoy it. We see another person in another body and have communion on all kinds of levels, from intensive love to friendly relationships in work or recreation.

We lay this physical frame on a bed at night and go to sleep—whatever that is—and awaken with mind and body restored, refreshed and revitalised. We energise it with food, and automatically breathe air. The blood circulates, food is digested and millions of new cells are created in a ceaseless stream. Apart from conscious thinking and attention to basic needs like food, sleep, exercise and cleanliness, the whole system is self-maintained and is activated outside our conscious control.

Countless books have been written on the mechanisms of the physical body. The more we discover about our bodies, the more marvellous do we see them to be. It is as though an Almighty Intelligence were working within us, always creating and re-creating tissues and organs, and performing a million intricate operations in minute detail.

We have even begun to understand some of the ways in which our computer-like brains function, and how the intricate network of nerves transmits commands to every part of our organism. New research uncovers the mysteries of the genes and chromosomes and the coded patterns which pre-determine and control the orderly creation of the body from its beginning as the union of male and female cells in the womb.

No wonder we pause in awe before this miraculous machine in which we function. Here, at least, we can observe and evaluate much of what is taking place in the endless chain of action and creativeness.

Less easy to understand and assess is the real you! Yet this is where the great miracle is to be found. Beyond all the marvels of the physical body are the incredible, intangible powers of the mind.

What are you? Body—or mind? One truth is clear: the body can do nothing without the mind which indwells and motivates it. When we reach the experience of death we simply see a body from which "life" or "mind" has departed. There is now no power to give commands to the brain—to move, feel, touch, see, taste or smell.

So we must come back to the central truth about yourself. Your entire life, all that you have been and all that you are now is entirely confined to what you, as a mind, have observed, thought about, mentally motivated and reacted to in every experience.

Let us pause for a few moments and stand aside from our flesh. Imagine again that we are sitting together in your home. Thank you for fellowship with me. Shall we settle down for a chat? You are sitting opposite me—or at least, I see your body relaxing in a chair. But where are YOU?

Your thoughts are reaching me shaped in words, and through the expression on your face. I perceive something of the real you in your eyes, your smile, and the impact of your personality. We are friends—together—and know our communion mainly through our conscious appreciation of each other's presence. We know this only by mental processes. Two dead bodies sitting in the same chairs would have no contact whatever.

Lift your arm. How did you do it? Wiggle your toes, move your body, speak. Look across the room—what do you see and how do you see it? The light from each object certainly reaches your eyes and you have the scene in focus. The light impulse is transformed in the eye into tiny electrical currents which flash along the nerves to the brain and activate cells there. Then what?

Perhaps we could define the brain as a computer which receives and stores impressions and presents them, as on a screen, to an observer. You, the invisible mind, the life, stand supreme in the midst of brain and body, and interpret the impressions presented to you. You focussed on the room; and this impression, linked with memories of countless similar impressions of rooms, gives a picture which you now assess, understand and recognise.

Similarly with all the other senses with which your form, or body, is endowed. Still sipping your tea? Feel the warm cup, taste the refreshing liquid in your mouth. The signals travel like lightning to your brain and YOU enjoy the sensations of the heat and taste of tea.

Be quiet for a few moments. Close your eyes and listen to every sound. A clock is ticking; a car is passing in the street; a dog barks; my slow breathing in the chair opposite is heard; some children call outside; a bird sings in the garden.

Every sound travels through the air as a vibration, and impinges on your ears. Each vibration, on a wavelength attuned to the noise, flashes its electric messages along the nerves from ear to brain, and your mind, *now paying attention to sounds*, interprets and recognises each one according to its memory of similar sounds in the past.

All things we understand or interpret in the mind depend on our attention to them. We decide, constantly, what we wish to experience. For instance, quite probably while we were talking we would not even have heard the sounds of clock, children, car, dog or bird. Our attention was focussed on each other, and on the verbal thoughts we were exchanging.

If during our conversation a jet plane flying overhead broke through the sound-barrier with its characteristic "boom", our minds would instantly switch startled attention to the noise and no doubt we would exclaim, "What's that!"

Now, retreat into your inner self for a few moments. Recognise your body as an instrument which you, as a mind, control and indwell. You are a mind, a life, a spirit. But at the same time you are real; you know your sense of identity; you are alive. Feel this sense of power, of control, of independence from the body as such.

Be quiet for a few minutes and fully appreciate the significance of this simple truth. You are experiencing the fact of BEING a mind, a spirit, and are poised in complete control of your body; all-powerful in your ability to direct your life as you choose.

*   *   *

Who are *you*? You don't know—not in the highest and intangible sense of definition. But you do know, precisely, that you exist, that you remember countless events of past experience, and that you are aware of your present identity.

You have now taken the greatest single step forward in vital knowledge if you have understood, completely and forever, that you are a spirit, a mind, endowed with eternal life, dwelling temporarily in a body which you use, control and dominate like a precision instrument for your physical contact with your present material environment.

This means, quite simply, that you can divorce yourself from much slavery to the body and even from the difficulties of everyday life. Your attention should now become focussed on your real power, as a mind, to appreciate and mould your environment according to your choice. Life is basically a *mental* experience with infinite creative possibilities.

From now on let us talk together with this concept clearly in, and always central to, our thoughts. Then we can discover, together, so many of our latent creative potentials and see how best we can use them to advance our way of life in sequences of multiplying good.

Where do you come from? Who really knows the heights and depths of such a mystery? But at least we can marvel at the truth of your being—for here you are! When those two living cells from your mother and father fused as one, the plan and pattern of your life proceeded forthwith to unfold. And all this took place through a *planned* infusion of life. There has to be a Thinker before anything can be created—so you owe your life to the universal Creator Who shared His purposes with your earthly parents.

Where are you going? Who knows precisely? But we certainly know that life is not matter and that you are not a body, even though you indwell one and use it. You are life, mind, spirit—beyond definition. You are part of eternal energy, the substance of reality, an eternal being destined to reveal the infinite potentials of consciousness in realms here and beyond.

We shall explore many aspects of mind and personality as we proceed. As we share each one we shall move, concept by concept, into a much clearer understanding of ourselves and, therefore, quicken some of the infinite powers that lie dormant within us all, awaiting recognition and direction.

You can be sure of one all-pervading truth. You are, at this moment, in your experience and personality, the product of all your thoughts since you were born, plus some essence of the heritage of your forebears and of the human race. What you are to become in the future will be conditioned and fashioned by your prevailing thoughts and attitudes of mind, through daily application and reaction to your experiences.

How vital it is that we learn to develop our inborn faculty for creative, imaginative and positive thinking! Then all things become possible. What man can conceive, he can achieve.

Let us continue this personal exploration in a true spirit of adventure. It is the most rewarding and exciting project to which we can ever devote our attention. It deals with the only asset any one of us can *ever* possess— our lives! It shows us the way our lives can best be unfolded to promote our highest and eternal good, and ultimately the final destiny of mankind.

But before pointing out the tremendous powers of

your mind when it is concentrated upon any given objective, which I intend to outline in the next chapter, I should like you to absorb the Power Thoughts detailed below.

POWER THOUGHTS

1 You are a spirit, manifesting through MIND, temporarily indwelling a body which is an instrument you use, through consciousness, to contact your environment.

2 Develop the practice of being aware of your MIND as the invisible, real YOU. Recognise every action of the body, and the events of the day, as originating in the mind.

3 Hold the truth that thoughts are living things which express, for good or ill, according to their positive or negative quality and intensity.

YOUR MIGHTY MIND

For as he thinketh in his heart, so is he.—PROVERBS 23: 7.

Ye deaf to Truth, midst error's clamorous din
Heed now the message of the Power within.
Look forth and see, ye spiritually blind,
The depth and outreach of your wondrous Mind;
No goal too nebulous, no aim too high—
Vast as the ocean, boundless as the sky

Soar ever upward, through celestial air,
On to the mountain-peaks of answered prayer.
Affirm your heritage and turn Faith's key

Releasing your dynamic destiny.
You are invincible! His Light before
Shines, as you operate Love's mystic lore.

*   *   *

Strength for the seeking, dreams Divinely true,
Wait in th' immortal Mind God gave to you.
"MAC"

Chapter 3

THOUGHTS ARE LIVING THINGS

A T THE VERY centre of the mind is its awareness of self, as an entity, a personality, the "I am", and its recognition of the environment throughout each conscious moment of every day.

We live in an inward world of the mind, but the "outward" scene is presented in an insistent flow of pictures and events to which we react both as observers and participants. We are so accustomed to this acceptance of the outward appearance of reality that we seldom realise that even the scene we contemplate is, in truth, a *mental* interpretation of it.

What we see, or become aware of, depends entirely on our choice and the degree of concentration we apply to it.

Imagine two people walking through a beautiful park. One man is consumed with worry about his business and a big decision he must make during the day; it will determine his future course perhaps for years ahead. He walks among the trees, and the path winds down to the lake. The sun is shining and the birds are singing. Spring flowers are blooming everywhere and it is a perfect morning.

He is aware of the park and of the general direction he is taking. But his mind observes little of the details of the beautiful scene. About eighty per cent of his attention is on his problems and he is scarcely aware of his walk through the park.

The other man, walking the same way, has his entire attention focussed on the park and the unfolding scene as he passes through it. He breathes the fresh spring air and it feels so good. He appreciates the sunshine, the shadows and the patterns of light among the trees. Daffodils catch his eye and he marvels at their beauty. Each tree and bush, the sweeping green lawns, the lake, quacking ducks, the flight and song of birds, and a thousand other exquisite details delight his mind as he absorbs them all.

I merely seek here to illustrate the importance of our awareness, and to emphasise that every experience is unfolded in our minds. The first man was concentrating on his problems; the second on his immediate environment; and both were evolving the mental patterns of their choice.

Our purpose for the moment is to establish complete agreement that we all function as *minds* because, as we unfold together the infinite capacities we possess, this central concept is fundamental to our objective. Only from this basic understanding can we fully exercise our wonderful gifts of love, imagination, will power, concentration and positive thinking. Only then can we fully appreciate the significance of our even greater outreach as spiritual beings living in a spiritual universe, and our ability to quicken and implement our highest destiny.

I am writing these words in my caravan, parked in a woodland glade. Why not come and join me here? Come inside. You are now sitting beside me on this beautiful morning. Although there was a slight frost overnight the sun is streaming through the windows with a warm glow

which tells us spring will soon be here. Comfortable?
Relax on the cushions and look outside.

The trees all round us are still quite bare of leaves but
the young buds show points of green. The tufted grass
stretches among the trunks and bushes, and the brown
winter patches are quickening with new green
growth. Oh look! That flight of starlings swarming and
as one landing in the glade! They are pecking in
the sweet grasses—and now, following some unheard
signal, they fly off in a cloud pattern, fluttering in the
sunshine.

Listen! Sparrows chirruping in those bushes. A subdued
roar of traffic in the distance. No wind. The slender
branches pointing to the sky in the great stillness. Can
you hear the silence? Can you see those pools of water
on the path with a sheen of new ice on the surface? Hoar
frost still lingering in the shadow of the trees. Blue sky.
The warm sun.

So here we are, together, aware of our material environment. In our minds we accept the picture and agree in a
general way about the place where we are now stopping.
Now let us probe a little deeper into some of the details
of the scene.

Look at the trees and the grass. What are they? Yes—
mental impressions, but they also exist in their own right.
They, too, are not quite what they seem to be because
within each tree and blade of grass is the invisible power
which creates and maintains them. Let us go out into the
field.

I grasp a handful of grass, roots and soil. The old stems
are brown, the new ones a vivid green, looking so slender
and alive. Chew one of these young shoots. Taste the
sweet sap. There are two or three hundred blades in my

handful, seemingly twisted and knotted together but revealing the pattern of luxuriant growth.

Astonishing is the mass of roots! More roots than green grass with thousands of delicate hair-like fibres which a moment ago were searching in the soil for sustenance. A tiny ant and a little wet worm have wriggled out of them! And now, look again; quite a number of the smallest worms I have ever seen—no thicker than the fibrous roots—are twisting their pale bodies as they adjust to the disturbance we caused by plucking the grass from the ground.

And just smell this cluster! Isn't the mixture of grass, roots and damp soil exquisite? It breathes life and reminds me of happy hours lying in a grassy meadow in summer sunshine, breathing deeply, and listening to the drone of bees and the song of birds.

What makes it grow? There is obviously a very intricate pattern involved in its creation. A seed—an invisible plan stamped within it. An inbuilt ability to rest in the soil; under the impulse of sunshine and rain it thrusts roots into the substance of the soil and shoots upwards into the air. This involves the multiplication of millions of cells as they create new cells, each in its correct order and for its planned functions. There is a principle involved because a definite and observable action takes place. What, or who, can produce a blade of grass?

The roots draw water and vital chemicals from the soil; these are transformed into sap (or grass blood) which reaches every part and is food for the cells as they increase in growth. The blades absorb energy from the sun and air and, in due season, produce the seeds which again contain the creative pattern and power for new grass to multiply according to its kind.

Those worms we have been observing! What an amazing work they do! If, by some catastrophe, all the worms in the world suddenly died, all vegetation and all life on the planet would soon cease to exist. Praise the humble worm and its endless labours in the cosmic scheme!

Consider this tuft of grass. A commonplace thing—but it clothes the earth and, in its various forms, feeds the animals, birds and man. No grass—no world as we know it.

I think of picturesque farms, green hills and meadows, grazing cows, rabbits and geese, birds in their millions, woodland glades, swirling grasses on the edge of a mountain stream, tall tropical shoots and close-cropped lawns, new spring grass and the sunburnt golden hills of California. Happy days helping with the haymaking on a farm. Warm, glorious days, sweating in the fields and forking the cut grass. The clank of the cutting machines, the roar of tractors and trucks. Break for tea and sandwiches with the men happily resting in the deep grass in the hedge. The happy face of the farmer when the last bundle of hay goes on to the top of the haystack. Winter feed for the cattle now in the barn. The green grass which was in the field retaining its life-giving qualities long after the summer sunshine has gone.

My friend, as we carefully replace this root and come back to my caravan, let us consider our exploration of this minute part of our scene. Wasn't it interesting? Why? Because we turned our minds away from the general environment to concentrate on one small part of it. This brought into operation several unique qualities of consciousness. First, we chose a handful of grass on which to meditate. Secondly, we directed our bodies, legs and hands to secure the object which we desired to consider. Thirdly, our *interest* in the experiment focussed mental concentration to evoke ideas concerning it. Fourthly, visual aid produced the impressions of what we were observing. And finally, these impressions blended with our memory of past experience and knowledge about many aspects of grass and its function.

A principle of mind is that for as long as we contemplate any chosen object it will release information about itself, and will evoke all our knowledge and associated ideas about it which give us a very comprehensive understanding. In a short time we have probably learned more about grass than we ever knew before simply because we became identified more closely with it through close concentration. Even so, the ideas that came to us are still only a fraction of what we could discover should we care to delve deeper and read all the knowledge man has collected through research. And beyond that still lie the invisible life forces and patterns and laws which are fundamental to its purposeful existence.

As we journey on we shall discuss many ways whereby the various qualities of the mind can be stimulated to produce a deeper, richer and more creative way of life. But, since everything we experience depends on the central fact of awareness of self, as a receptive and motivating mind, it is interesting and vital to deepen this understanding.

Keep this truth before you. What we have just done is a simple way to this end. As often as you can each day pause to remember your self as pure consciousness, and absorb the outward scene as an inward observer. Everything, without exception, contains within itself information which your mind can awaken and contemplate. The thoughts which arise will always bring you joy and an exciting reminder of the power of your own being.

Even if you are lonely, sick or isolated from the thrust of human affairs the immediate scene is pulsating with power and information. Or, as you go about your daily work, everything you see, touch or experience is alive and awaiting your keener appreciation. There is nothing of the commonplace about you as an individual, or about the world and people round you—whatever your circumstances.

Consider even simple things. A box of matches can swiftly take you into the realm of form, factories, shipping, timber in the forests, fire and a hundred other facts. A flower, from petal to root, will reveal its beauty and purpose. The gold ring on your finger will awaken memories of relationships, gold mines and miners, jewellers and finance. From wool rugs to sheep on the moorland, clothing to weavers and tailors, electric light to inventors and power stations. The list is endless.

Apart from realising the fascinating fund of information which is there for the asking in every kind of environment we are learning the basic art of concentration; and when we later add our special gifts of love and imagination we shall find a new and infinite scope for creating and achieving every true objective. All our higher qualities cannot emerge into full expression unless we constantly realise that the mind is the basic power through which our *total* life experience is being created.

Because we are so involved with the body, as outlined when I sat with you in your room, it would be well now to increase this awareness by practising the following process. Using the same method we shared when contemplating the tuft of grass, spend some time every day considering each part of your physical system. The purpose here is, of course, to establish yourself completely as an entity, the "I am", in control of those functions given into your conscious care, and the "I am" indwelling your bodily mechanism.

Concentrate on the flexing and stretching of your many muscles. Get the "feel" of them as *you* instruct their motivation. Breathe deeply—and consider the purpose of breath. Look at your fingers and evoke all the thoughts and memories you can about your hand. Then your legs, eyes, ears, mouth. This is the Real You coming into closer accord with your physical body and its amazing functions.

What makes you laugh or cry? Always something which affects your mind. How do you stand, or walk? Consider how the body could do neither by itself. In fact, the two small feet of bone and flesh and the top-heavy body could not even stand up on their own. So the mind is the power which helps you to balance your physical frame.

Perhaps some part of your body is not functioning correctly. Perhaps you are ill in bed, growing old, or incapacitated in some way? If so, it is possible you have accepted the idea that the body cannot function as it should do. I am fully aware, of course, with deep compassion and understanding, that sickness in all its forms takes a terrible toll and limits our lives and minds, but it is still true that much can be done to help heal and alleviate these troubles; we shall consider this in more detail later on. Meanwhile let it be said again that your central experience is always in consciousness. The sick body? Yes, even that, because it is the mind which has become aware of the sickness and interprets it for what it is.

It is always, therefore, an important step towards well-being if you can consistently recognise and accept the truth that the real YOU is a spirit, a mind, in charge of the physical system. The body is built to obey your mental commands and impulses. I say to my hand "Move" and it moves; it has no power to do so under its own volition. Whatever the mind accepts becomes "real" to it. And if it believes completely in the prevailing physical sickness or limitation it is surrendering its authority. Better to work constantly towards affirming health, strength, and vitality towards every part of the body.

We shall discuss the destructive effects of negative beliefs and thought patterns in some detail, but it is a good start to re-establish your central authority and to deepen your recognition of the power of your mind over your body. Positive thinking always involves evoking the "patterns of the perfect" in relation to every experience. So the more surely you are able to abandon the "picture" of the sickness or disability and replace it with a secure and prevailing belief in health and perfect everything, the sooner will your body respond to this healthy image.

It is a good plan, if specific members of the body are not functioning correctly, to re-mobilise them gently and without strain by practising whatever movements are within your capabilities. Seek consciously and with deep conviction to make some advance in mobility each day, and be constant in an over-all awareness of perfect health.

Your entire focus will then be on your true self and on your dominion over every physical organism. You will certainly feel stronger, freer and more sure of yourself as you extend this awareness of your positive-thought processes. Then, too, your attitude to medical attention will change. You will be much more able to co-operate with doctors and nurses who are seeking to help you. Your whole being will then gather up all its real strength to assist those who are helping you in a drive towards wholeness.

So all joy to you today. I behold you going forward into every spiritual-mental adventure for your highest good. In this deeper awareness of your greater being, new strength flows to you and your confidence and peace of mind will embrace and inspire everyone whose life touches yours.

We now move to the next step when we will discuss the real YOU, your character and personality, but before doing so I should like you to dwell upon the following Power Thoughts:

POWER THOUGHTS

1 Whenever you, as a Mind, consider any subject, situation or object, ideas and knowledge related to it will at once flow to your awareness.

2 Take a loaf of bread and set it before you. Quietly let the bread tell you a sequence of facts about itself. Trace these fascinating thoughts from shape and texture right through to wheatfields, mills, farmers, bakers and your own personal experiences.

3 Consider the events in which you participated yesterday. Begin at the moment of awakening and follow through your movements, contacts, and the thoughts you motivated in relation to each experience. And recognise those thoughts or mental attitudes which were negative and positive respectively.

4 Look at your room, another person, or a scene outside and deepen your understanding that you are observing everything entirely in your MIND.

THE DIVINE THINKER

How precious also are thy thoughts unto me, O God! how great is the sum of them!—PSALM 139: 17.

The stars are fading and the galaxy
Is hidden 'neath the dawn's pale robe of blue;
Raising my head in dazzled awe I see
The heavens tapestried in rainbow hue.
God's musings gleam like crystal on the grass,
His feathered fancies carol as they pass.

From Springtide's tender bud to Summer's rose,
There steals a whisper of His mystic Plan;
Weaving a web celestial it goes
O'er Nature's pathways to encompass man.
Beside a tideless, tranquil lake I lie
And watch God's jewelled thoughts drift gently by.

Moment by fretful moment I am hurled
Through the incessant whirlpool of the world,
Yet lift my gaze and in an instant know
The purpose of this life, with His aglow.

*   *   *

I AM A THOUGHT OF GOD. Oh, may I be
Worthy the Mind Divine that pondered me.
                                    "MAC"

Chapter 4

THE POWER OF PERSONALITY

OUR THOUGHTS, so far, have been concentrating on determining that we are, first and foremost, spiritual-mental beings experiencing life in our bodies in an environment which we accept, recognise and interpret.

May I now come and join you so that we can talk about the real YOU, your character and personality? We can at least do this in imagination. I can visualise a picture of you—man or woman—and at the same time you are receiving thoughts from my mind and personality. We are communicating with one another, and this fact of being is fundamental to every aspect of life. We do not, and cannot live as self-contained entities. Inevitably we share this planet with some three thousand million people, and we are all interwoven in consciousness and are dependent in some degree on the thoughts and actions of everyone else.

We can observe that for we possess an individual personality, and this is woven into the framework of a family, a social group, a nation and the world. The very diversity of every aspect of personality is the sign of the illimitable potential inherent in mankind. Every person, every group and every nation is different one from the other within the basic pattern of humanity.

But there is only one YOU! In all the vast multitudes of people living on earth at this time—only one YOU. Indeed, the modern astronomer would seem to confirm the overwhelming possibility that the infinite universe, with all its billions of galaxies, is teeming with life on all levels of evolution. Yet even among all these potentially uncountable billions of beings—there is still only one YOU and only one ME!

You resemble a piece of a jigsaw puzzle. The picture cannot be completed without you; and whatever is your perfect pattern, your true contribution to life, only *you* can create and express it, now and forever.

I find great strength in this truth because it leads me to appreciate the vital power inherent in every individual. It inspires an absolute reverence for life because I can only accept, humbly and completely, that such a miracle as a human being could certainly not be produced by some haphazard blending of chemical components. The very pattern of a personality, with its incredible mind and complicated body, confirms the power and purpose of a Creator who planned it all. No scientist could do that!

It violates all reason even to begin to think of a universe of law and order, in all its illimitable grandeur down to the tiniest exquisite detail, without totally accepting the fact of an Almighty Mind which planned and maintains it. That is why it is impossible to discuss human personality without relating it to people with whom we associate, to the world family, and also to our involvement in universal creation. We are necessarily subject to the laws which govern the universe. We are part of it all, and wisdom decrees a search for those factors of personality, as far as we can discern them, which come into harmony with the central purposes of life.

But let us talk about YOU. What is your true personality like? What kind of impression do other people have of you? All that you are depends on your experiences in the past, your reactions to them, and your basic attitudes to people and events now. It is not easy to evaluate your own personality for you cannot see yourself as objectively as can an observer, but you have a memory and can quickly assess your qualities and attitudes when you honestly start to analyse them.

Perhaps we can best approach the question by deciding what we agree to be a good personality. We have a surprising ability to discern what we deem to be good or bad in other people, and we certainly react very strongly to the characteristic behaviour of others.

We have no difficulty in appreciating a loving, kind and tolerant nature. Whenever we see someone who is generous, friendly, ever seeking to help in all situations, we at once recognise these fine qualities. We are stimulated by courage and confidence, trustworthiness and steadfast loyalty in the midst of difficulties. We respect and admire the man or woman who is unselfish, understanding and compassionate towards others. We like to see faith and every spiritual quality being expressed in the home, at work and at play.

We equally recognise and dislike personalities that emanate negative thoughts—fear, worry, tension, anger, irritability and bitterness. Unloving personalities always repel, and our inward nature too easily condemns the "wrongdoer", often without pausing to realise that we can never know enough about anyone else to be able justly to judge and condemn.

We are, each of us, mainly the expression of our thinking and our reactions to the sum total of our experiences from childhood. It is a simple truth that we are all like children learning how to live with our complex mind and its relationships with other people. And, as we all know, we *each* have our good qualities and failings.

Some have suffered more than others; some have had an easier passage. Ignorance and shocks in childhood have sometimes warped a personality. Discordant relationships have broken many lives. Injustice, wars and economic tribulations in an evolving and as yet imperfect society, affect everyone to a greater or lesser degree.

But *you are* the person we are considering. Whoever you are, your presence, thinking and nature always affect the people around you. And equally, you are constantly reacting, for good or ill, to everyone with whom you associate.

It is always important, therefore, to know your true self and to seek by every means to eliminate faults and achieve the most balanced, poised and positive personality you can imagine. How to do this? Before we can even begin to change anything, we must be aware of the need and then deliberately take the necessary compensating steps.

Honesty with self is essential, otherwise the need is simply glossed over by that very comforting ego of the mind which will try to justify every self-expression. No matter who you are, even if you had free choice, you would *never* exchange your life for that of someone else. So you are YOU, and it is your eternal purpose to evolve the highest, the noblest and the best.

I, too, am learning much about myself as I write these words. I am sure we shall both be better people when we have finished our discussions! Self-examination is never easy but most essential.

Let me assure you that there is one fundamental power within us which, when fully understood and expressed, gives us the perfect "key" to successful living and the "Power Thinking" personality through which we can achieve every worthy objective. It is so simple that it is often overlooked or only partly recognised. It is, indeed, a power so transcendental in operation that it is all-embracing, and so easy to develop that it sweeps every other mental ability into one central and effective manifestation.

Keep this in mind as we continue to discuss your personality, because in our next session we shall bring this power to the forefront of all our objectives. We are now simply preparing the way for our acceptance of it by recognising the truth of our mental being and the personality through which all our thoughts, attitudes and actions are expressed.

Remember, please, that it is not our purpose to embark on a complicated course of mind training, but rather to awaken those latent powers within the reach of everyone. And, because you are receiving these thoughts, every concept offered has a deep significance for you. Truth is sometimes so simple that it is hard to accept.

So, without getting too involved will you pause to assess your true personality, as far as you can? You will know, with a little thought, most of your good qualities and weaknesses. Let me provide you with just a few questions which may help you. It will be most helpful, for your personal analysis, if you write down, briefly, your honest answers.

Are you happy, content with your present position in life? If not, why? Do people like you? Do you mix well with others? Are you loving, kind, generous and tolerant in your relationships? What problems exist in your home? If you are married, are you happy with each other, and with your family? If not, what is the true nature of the difficulty? Are you doing your best to be patient, compassionate, and understanding with those close to you? What *are* the qualities in which you excel?

Are you inclined to worry about your problems? Are you selfish, irritable, bitter, or upset about anything? Are you sick? Do you know the cause of the trouble? Are you lonely? What are your weaknesses? Are you frustrated in your vocation? Why? Why?

Decide what interests you most in life. What creative gifts do you best express? Are you successful in your work? Do you like it? Are you achieving your objectives? What are they? What special qualities and knowledge do you possess which can be used to advance your vocation? If you had all power to accomplish it, what kind of a person would you like to be, as an individual, and in your job?

Do you believe in God? Have you faith in yourself and faith in prayer? Do you accept that spiritual principles promote our highest well-being and harmonise our relationships with others? These are the questions you must ask yourself.

*   *   *

It is always helpful to pause long enough to try and see yourself as others do. You can be quite sure that the people with whom you live and work, your friends and those whom you meet, will all have a contrasting image of your personality. They will assess your good qualities and your weaknesses, and adjust their relationships with you accordingly. Just as you, too, recognise the same characteristics in others.

Now, at least, you should have quickened the awareness

of your character. You should have a clearer idea of your assets and liabilities. And, therefore, you should now be able to increase the expression of your positive abilities and begin to overcome your weaknesses.

Everyone has an instinctive drive towards a happy, positive, creative way of life. Millions of us fail to achieve this objective because we do not understand the deeper meaning of life, the true and purposeful functions of our minds, or the necessity to obey the spiritual-mental laws which are fundamental to our highest and creative good.

We have become outstanding in complicated invention and material achievement; but we have still not understood the basic nature of man as a spiritual personality, and that he can fulfil himself only when his creative expression is linked with a balanced spiritual motivation.

The real danger to-day is lest we become self-sufficient in material possessions and intellectual ability, and are tempted to neglect the vital harmonies of the personality. We cannot live by bread alone, and if the mind is not fed and motivated by spiritual vision and purpose we create destructive tensions and discords which erupt in sickness, breakdown and unhappiness.

It is a significant and revealing truth that the main problems of the individual and the world are essentially spiritual ones. The tragic disasters of war represent hatred—the breaking of the Law of Love. It is not a political or a strategic problem, but at root purely a spiritual one. If by some miracle everyone on earth simultaneously accepted the principle of Love as absolute law, then wars and conflicts of all kinds would surely cease.

The healing of wars and human conflicts is a spiritual

objective. We may well be a long way from its realisation but, nevertheless, it is the enduring purpose of mankind to work for its ultimate achievement.

What has this to do with personality? Simply that we all form part of the whole, and that our first responsibility is always to begin with ourselves.

We know now through experience and research that all negative thoughts produce negative and, therefore, discordant experiences and often corresponding physical disturbances. Lack of love, expressed in intolerance, unforgiveness, bitterness, conflict and anger, brings only painful and often disastrous conditions in the mind, body and environment.

We all know this, of course, but the problem has always been how to find the remedy. Since all negative attitudes reveal some divergence from spiritual principles we cannot seriously find the answer until we accept and motivate consistently the spiritual laws of mind which govern the solution.

The power of positive thinking is also now well known, and many techniques have been invented to help people to achieve this power. But our purpose here is to concentrate on the basic gifts we all possess which can be used on command to remove all our weaknesses and surge into a creative expression which will encompass every aspect of our lives.

Let us now move confidently to this central concept, which I call "The Law of Multiplying Good", and know that wonderful things are in the making as we continue our exploration of mind. But let us first dwell on the following Power Thoughts:

Power Thoughts

1 In all the universe there is only ONE you! Everyone else, without exception, is also a unique being and personality in his or her own right.

2 As a personality you express the essence of your thoughts, mental attitudes and reactions to people and environment since you were born—plus those characteristics inherited from your forebears, and through the patterns of racial consciousness in which you live.

3 You can, therefore, develop your personality to express all those harmonious, happy, positive and creative qualities which you recognise to be worthy of your sustained interest and practice.

4 In quiet contemplation seek to evaluate your good qualities and also those which are distorted, weak or negative.

5 Trace some of the episodes in your life where your personality expressed negative qualities which disturbed you and upset others. And bring to awareness experiences where YOU brought about joy, constructive and creative events for your own well-being and for others.

6 Consider the kind of person you would truly yearn to become. And quicken your interest with decision to set this up as your high goal, knowing that concentration on it will surely create it.

YOU

Hereby ye shall know that the Lord hath sent me to do all these works; for I have not done them of mine own mind.
—NUMBERS 16: 28.

There is a special task to do
That no one can achieve but YOU.
There is a wondrous prayer to pray
That none save YOU can ever say.

A path of promise shines ahead
No other soul may ever tread;
A door into Eternity
To which YOU hold the only key.

God gives His works to countless men
To render back to Him again;
But none can weave YOUR pattern through
Because—He only made one YOU.

"MAC"

Chapter 5

THE LAW OF MULTIPLYING GOOD

MAY I NOW come into the garden of your mind and look, with you, at the most beautiful flowers you have cultivated over the years you have dwelt there? In this sense, consciousness is like a garden, and our thoughts are like seeds which grow and multiply according to their kind. And as in any cultivated ground, we find there a variety of beautiful creations—and also many weeds. But will you, the gardener, now show me your finest blooms? And tell me of those which you grew most successfully?

Imagine again that we are sitting together, two friends interested in each other and in our exchange of ideas, and the search for everything that is good, practical and beautiful. May I ask you about your greatest moments and share with you the happiness you found in creating them?

In your life there have been many situations which brought you joy and fulfilment. Think about them for a few minutes. Your memory is stored with these high moments and it is good, not only now but often, to spend quiet times re-living the delightful events which brought you happiness and creative achievement. But, when you do this, let your heart be filled with gratitude and not with regret at their passing. They are part of the garden of remembrance which you have created and are indelibly stamped on your personality. They are the roots which feed your mind and provide the power for even greater experiences now and in the eternal future.

As you bring these memories to mind you will at once recognise that these great events were all expressing LOVE in a multitude of exhilarating ways. Indeed, Love is the "Pearl of Great Price" for it radiates its power in as many ways as does personality.

You may remember the bliss of a loving mother caring for your needs, and the joy of your father sharing his life and experiences with you in your childhood. I hope so, for the greatest grief a child can ever know is when, for whatever reason, this love is denied or frustrated.

Pictures of happy friendships, as you played together with your brothers, sisters and friends, will "flash upon that inward eye which is the bliss of solitude." Picnics by the river, in the woods, or by the sea. Schooldays—your joy when you took your first drawing or writing home to mother. Do you remember the hobbies which captured your youthful interest—games, hiking, cycling, collecting flowers, stamps, loving dolls and making dresses for them, building towers with bricks, or creating trucks and bridges with a construction set? Christmas time—the gifts which thrilled you in the loving family circle?

In school you excelled at those subjects in which you were most interested. Perhaps you roamed the world in imagination during geography lessons, or wove your dreams into little stories you wrote in English classes. If mathematics captured your interest, how exciting it was to build those patterns of figures and equations! Or perhaps your very soul was lost in domestic science and tasty cooking, in philosophy or engineering, or later perhaps, medicine. Wherever your interest was concentrated, your creative enjoyment was at its highest and your work correspondingly good.

No doubt you can recall breath-catching memories of your first sweetheart in your teens. And, I am sure, all heaven seemed to flow to you. Life was good. The first days at the work of your choice. The excitement of feeling grown-up, a man in a man's world, or a woman in hers.

If you loved your work in the home, office, farm, factory or laboratory then you enjoyed its fellowship and creativeness. A way of life was unfolding with many experiences—some exquisite, and some quite devastating.

Courtship days—marriage—children? If this was your experience then much of it held periods of contentment and joy, according to the degree in which love was fully expressed.

Remember for the moment we are exploring all your peak periods of happiness and creative fulfilment. You will find that you have no difficulty at all in bringing those ecstasies and created works into focus now. And, of course, I can only hope that your present position is likewise blessed with infinite and multiplying good.

What I seek to illustrate is that every good, happy and creative experience was produced essentially through the action of Love expressing through your relationships with others, and by your interest, dedication, persistence and concentration (which are aspects of love) on the work of your choice.

Love is the Great Law of Life. It contains the secret of every aspect of the perfect personality, and the complete fulfilment of everything you ever seek to create in your home, at work and play, or plan for the future. It is the central and most important power in consciousness and the true dynamic of positive, creative, and imaginative Power Thinking.

Yet—how can one define this Power? Philosophers, spiritual leaders, poets and other thinkers have sought to express and understand its significant virtues. But it is infinite in its existence, completely beyond definition, intangible, all-powerful, mysterious, compulsive and, when fully flowing, transcends reason and intellect.

Although we cannot describe it we can, however, evaluate its action. It is a quality of being which every one has. And everyone has had experience of its efficacy.

Because it is a power beyond definition we have seldom recognised the all-pervading influence it exerts in every experience. When manifesting, it produces multiplying good; when absent, we are like lost souls wandering in the wilderness.

A strong statement? Let us see what we can discover about it. Let us relax. Comfortable? We are two spirits, two minds, poised in peace and contentment, just letting the love-thoughts flow. We are now interested to know all that love can tell us about itself. Our minds are focussed on it and, as in our diagnosis with the tuft of grass, we shall receive and share our impressions as they come to us. It is wonderful to be with you at this moment. I feel so close to you, so "at one" with you. Thank you for your fellowship and interest which make this possible.

Love? First let us consider the range of its expression. There is a modern tendency to think of it in a sentimental way. We more or less define it as a very beautiful quality which finds its highest expression between a married man and woman, with perhaps high moments of sexual communion, and in absorbing relationships with their children.

We have no difficulty at all in realising the joys inherent

in this situation. Some of our greatest moments and richest experiences are centred there. The bliss of a mother nursing her child with tender, loving care; the joy of a father. The patience, kindness, tolerance and comradeship of the home, when love illumines it, establish a high estate in the affairs of man.

We usually express these virtues in a somewhat lesser degree towards our special friends. But here, too, is a rich and rewarding experience.

Beyond these personal contacts we seem to lose sight of this Great Law. We tend to subscribe to the view that "sentiment", or love, has no part in the busy affairs of farm or factory. Business is business, and love belongs to the private realms of home and friendship. Still less do we associate it with our thought processes and our creative way of life.

The cost of this neglect is experienced throughout the world. So many broken and frustrated lives, so much selfishness, greed and intolerance, wars and personal conflicts; these tell the story, to all who can see the truth, of a failure to let love fulfil its purpose.

We need, urgently, to understand and accept that this is the basic law of creation, the basic creative power of life itself. Its purpose is to release its power into every thought, word and deed to create the highest expression of the personality and its objectives.

We talk much about concentration, will power, imagination and positive thinking in these enlightened days. We marvel constantly at the amazing creations of mankind through the efficient use of his imagination, intellect and multiplying knowledge. Yet we fail to realise that all these things have been accomplished through the use of the power of love through interest and imagination!

"Whatever the mind can conceive, it can achieve."
Yes—provided the imaginative concept is linked with the
creative power of Love. "But," you say, "they produced
these marvels through intellect and knowledge." True,
but only when the mind discovered an absorbing and
continuing *interest* in each project. Do you see? *Interest* is
love, and it was this power which concentrated the
constant flow of thoughts, which are living things indeed,
to the final accomplishment. When we *consciously* know
this truth we can cultivate this gift and increase its
effectiveness.

All projects are fulfilled in fellowship with other people.
Whether in a hospital or factory, laboratory or coal-mine,
home or office, farm or shop, we are absolutely dependent
on communion with our fellows, and the degree of our
harmony, interest and perseverance together will determine the final creative outcome.

We often assess the value of a business as "goodwill".
This reveals the degree of friendship and partnership
between the men and women who work in the organiza-
tion and the people who buy their products or services.
We know that many a business has failed when discords
and disputes have disrupted productivity; or when the
attitude of staff or management towards the customers has
been cold, hostile or careless.

Consider two workmen of equal capacity. One hates his
work. What do you find? A careless and disinterested
person, a weary worker longing to go home. His relationships with his fellows are poor, he is often unhappy,
negative in outlook, and his work is sub-standard. Indeed,
management will have assessed this and he is judged
accordingly.

The other loves every aspect and challenge of his job.

He radiates happiness, confidence and good fellowship. He sings at his work and finds joy in all he does. Management respects his integrity and marks him for promotion.

And so on right through the human scene. We discover the discords, tensions, weariness and lack of creative fulfilment wherever there is a lack of love for people, for work, or for our environment. Equally, a rewarding life is revealed wherever love is the motive.

I stress this harmonious power in its relation to our environment and the projects we are daily executing, for this is where the mind truly finds its full expression.

Whether we call it love, or interest, or concentration, matters little. What is important is our recognition of the truth that LOVE is the creative and motivating power of the mind, and that its flow or lack of expression, conditions our every experience.

By simple analysis we can say categorically that we cannot afford to hate anything or anyone. In varying degrees—disinterest, dislike, discords, irritability, worry, fear, frustration, intolerance, lack of forgiveness, and all negative attitudes produce unhappiness, failure and general disharmony of our innermost nature. And, as we know today, much physical sickness follows spiritual-mental disturbances.

I am not talking about sentimental love, but of the greatest power we possess. But I should here stress that in every experience this love is at its best when it is warm, glowing, and exuberant. In its own nature it is an emotion, but its power is restricted if we keep it in cold storage and seek to produce it as a cold intellectual quality.

At its finest it bursts forth as affection, enthusiasm, interest, warm and happy relationships; serving, giving of one's whole being for the good of the family, vocation, the community of the world. That is why we must bring it to a central point in our personalities. It is not enough to drift through life finding interest here, and lack of it there. We handicap ourselves by expressing this essential quality in haphazard ways, using it here and forgetting it there. Its all-embracing power is such that, if we value our happiness and health, we *must* cultivate this priceless gift, and boldly, joyously apply it to every aspect of living.

Let us pause for a few minutes. How good it is to be home! I have to travel in many countries in the course of my work, conducting services in churches of all denominations. I love every minute of it and cherish the kindness, hospitality and generosity of all the wonderful people I meet, and in whose homes I find fellowship and rest. But, oh, how good it always is to come home! You, too, will have had this experience whether you have been away on holiday or business. What a comfortable, warming experience it is to come back among family and friends and familiar things!

I suppose that for most of us it is in our home where we "recharge our batteries", so to speak, rest and make plans for the future. I am feeling this as I share this moment with you, and I am grateful for your warm fellowship with me as we "dream our dreams" together.

Perhaps we can now look at our love project from another angle. You will have a Bible on your shelves. Will you bring it? Thank you. Let us look at what I think to be the best statements about this law which have ever been proclaimed.

Jesus said: "The first of all commandments is: thou shalt love the Lord thy God with all thy heart, and with all thy soul, and with all thy mind, and with all thy strength.

"And the second is like, namely this, Thou shalt love thy neighbour as thyself. There is none other commandment greater than these."

In the light of modern knowledge about the causes of human disaster never has so vital a truth been given to man, with such emphasis, in so few words.

Then here are the words of St. Paul, in his profound letter to the Corinthians (1: 13):

"Though I speak with the tongues of men and of angels, and have not love, I am become as sounding brass, or a tinkling cymbal.

"And though I have the gift of prophecy, and understand all mysteries, and all knowledge; and though I have all faith, so that I could remove mountains, and have not love, I am nothing.

"And though I bestow all my goods to feed the poor, and though I give my body to be burned, and have not love, it profiteth me nothing.

"Love suffereth long, and is kind; love envieth not; love vaunteth not itself, is not puffed up.

"Doth not behave itself unseemly, seeketh not her own, is not easily provoked, thinketh no evil.

"Rejoiceth not in iniquity, but rejoiceth in the truth;

"Beareth all things, believeth all things, hopeth all things, endureth all things.

"Love never faileth: but whether there be prophecies, they shall fail; whether there be tongues, they shall cease; whether there be knowledge, it shall vanish away. . . .

"And now abideth faith, hope, love, these three; but the greatest of these is love."

And finally:

"For what shall it profit a man, if he shall gain the whole world, and lose his own soul?"—Mark 8: 36.

Here at least we have the ultimate definition of this Great Law, and the way in which we are invited to express it. It confirms and amplifies all that I have been trying to say to you.

But you and I are very practical people, and would not subscribe to anything that could not be usefully expressed in our lives. Would you like to experiment on your own? Let us call it a personal-research project—it sounds important—and, of course, it is!

Every valid experiment fulfils its purpose only if we follow exactly all the laws which control its unique pattern. If you were in a laboratory, intent on producing some chemical reaction following a particular formula, any deviation from the set specification would ruin your results. Likewise with the Great Law—it works, without fail, exactly according to the degree and accuracy to which we apply it in any given situation.

You may have had already some reservations about your ability to love your work if you dislike it; to forgive someone who wrecked your life in the past; to respect someone who dominates you—and so on. But wait!

For our purpose let us abandon these personal difficulties and set out with the firm conviction that, as we evoke love in every situation, we shall experience the fruits.

Take first your home as your focal point. Do you like it? Or what do you dislike about it? Switch on the power of love, and deliberately consider everything you can find that is good. Then, item by item, declare your love and gratitude for the good you can see in those things which you dislike. The good *is* always to be found if love directs your thoughts. And remember, some people do not even have a roof over their heads.

If you are a housewife you may dislike cleaning, washing up the dishes, or preparing the food, shopping, and all the chores which make a woman's life an endless task. Even so try spending one full day just loving everything you have to do. *Feel* an identity with the work, and love it as a privilege to clean and create, and if others are involved, to do it all with reverence and care for their sakes.

Very soon you will feel the joy surging through your being and begin to marvel how quickly the work gets done. You will probably sing while washing up the dishes, feel exalted in your creation of a new dish, and rejoice in the fresh beauty you are creating in your home. The shopping? You will find a new interest in your purchases, and your happy spirit will captivate the shop assistants and the people you meet.

When the day is done you will be happy, content, fulfilled. Tired? Amazingly you will feel alive and strong. Love multiplies the power expended and returns to you in peace of mind as you relax in the evening.

If you have to travel to office or factory, determine that this day will be devoted to service with joy in all you have to do. Give yourself with loving attention to people and your work. You will be astonished at all the new facets which will flow into expression, and the warm relationship you experience with those you are serving or meeting.

Most of our difficulties arise through unhappy relationships. In your case, whether at home or work, is there anyone who upsets you? What are your resentments? Is there anyone who has hurt you in the past, or who is

c

disturbing your life now? Face it all squarely and honestly on the understanding that if you are holding any bitterness, anger, or hatred against anyone you are not only thrusting him or her further into trouble, but also destroying your true self.

Not easy you say? Of course not, but a balanced mind demands action to break free from such crippling bondage. Begin with every opportunity and, instead of seeing weaknesses, mistakes or sins in those involved, dwell on the good you can find. At the same time realise that if others have hurt you, you too, at some time, have hurt them. We are all learning how to live and the weaker members among us are really inviting our strength to help them. This you can give only by love—expressed as kindness, tolerance, confidence and ever-willing help. And, above all, absolute and unconditional forgiveness.

Will you try? This is the first step, and you will be thrilled at the immediate blessings which will flow back to you in personal joy, freedom, peace and power; and you will also see a corresponding change in those you are now loving. Remember, too, that beyond the weakness in others you can always reverence the true life that, as in you, is in process of unfolding in them.

Whatever and whoever you hate or dislike—direct your love and you will have your reward. Even if you are sick in body, it is good to *love* the stricken parts. Bless each organ for the great work it has done so well down the years. Cherish your body and give positive thoughts to its well-being.

There is no episode in any day to which love cannot be deliberately directed. *Feel its power—it is warm, vibrant. It flows into consciousness not as thought, but as the power which transforms the thinking processes into constant positive expression.*

This is the real and simple secret of the Law of Love. For too long we have split the mind into qualities like memory, intellect, reasoning ability, will power and imagination, and sought by many devices to strengthen them by discipline and practice. We make hard work of what is in fact a natural creative process—when we know the secret.

Love, consistently expressed, must change the quality of our thinking. It transforms negative attitudes into positive expression. It produces harmony, health and well-being. It is interest and enthusiasm, and focusses the mind in deep concentration. It sweeps the imagination to its highest vision and opens the way to distant horizons.

We all know that concentration and application bring forth the results we seek. But it is only love which makes *effortless* concentration possible. The only discipline required is to recognise and accept that this is the fundamental Law, and then to apply it steadfastly. The results will astonish you! But remember—love is not mind. It is the mysterious essence of all creation, the power which infuses consciousness with its ability to think and create.

It is said, "God is Love." How well we can believe it when we see the marvels it produces when even we, as small sparks, can illumine our lives and achievements so wonderfully when we are centred in that knowledge.

The Great Law brings union and communion with one another. It is infectious and never fails to leave its mark wherever it is directed. It is the Law of Multiplying Good because whenever expressed it transforms our own lives, and all whose lives touch ours; and this, in turn, flows into an endless sequence of multiplying good works.

So much more could be said, for Love can be applied

to as many situations as there are. But I am sure you will have absorbed enough to see how you can use this power of Love in *your* life.

Let us now consider the next step. In our next talk let us look at the Power of Imagination. We shall then see how this central Law of Love affects and motivates our minds and their various qualities.

I behold you poised and centred in LOVE—the kindest, gentlest person anyone could ever wish to meet. You are now tolerant, understanding, compassionate and confident. You are a source of joy and inspiration, courage and faith to everyone you meet. You are a Power Thinker, able to achieve all that you desire.

POWER THOUGHTS

1 Love is the great Law of Multiplying Good. It is the Creative Power which transforms personality to its highest level. It floods the mind and transforms negative into positive thinking. It is the key to every aspect of creative achievement, to peace, happiness, health and well-being.

2 Your day will be according to your acceptance of this Law in good will, consideration, enthusiasm and service to your family, friends, fellow-workers and other people.

3 True Love is ENERGY. It replenishes the mind and body whenever selflessly released.

4 Daily deepen your awareness of this truth by evoking this "miracle law" in every situation. You will find the results will fall into two categories: (a) an immediate positive response to yourself and others; (b) increasing harmony as its multiplying power steadily adjusts any difficult situation at home or outside.

LET ME BE LOVE

Father, I am Thy child, and as Thy child I seek only to love,
to Bless and to serve all Thy children everywhere.
—BROTHER MANDUS.

I am Thy child, dear Father.   I will share
My Blessings with Thy children everywhere;
Seeking to serve and comfort all I meet,
Even as the Master cleansed His brethren's feet.

I will go out into the world to-day
Shedding Thy Spirit's glory on my way;
The channel of Thy message unto men
That Christ, their Healer, walks earth's paths again.

I am Thy child, dear Father. I will take
Thy solace to the lonely; for Thy sake
I become Love to all, that all may see
Thy benedictions mirrored forth in me.

"MAC"

Chapter 6

THE POWER OF CREATIVE IMAGINATION

WHEN TWO FRIENDS sit together conversation flows effortlessly between them. Fluid ideas are clothed with words following the subject of their attention, and new thoughts are stimulated by questions. Thus we probe and share each other's experiences. Such discussion usually has the merit of natural simplicity, and each seeming complexity is soon cleared by explanation.

That is why I want to establish this kind of relationship with you. To the extent that we are just two ordinary people seeking the simplest approach to the complexities of our personalities, so shall we continue to concentrate on the most essential points.

We could very quickly become bewildered by the countless definitions which philosophers and psychologists have proclaimed. We can accept, of course, their considerable contributions to the understanding of human nature, and be thankful that their discoveries flow into increasingly effective manifestation in the medical sciences, social services, industry and education.

Our purpose, however, is to concentrate on those spiritual-mental faculties which *everyone* can understand and immediately implement to increase every aspect of well-being and creativeness. It is, indeed, a "short cut" through to central and dynamic powers which we all possess, but usually express in a fluctuating and often haphazard way.

So far, to recapitulate, we have considered several basic factors which are absolutely essential to the higher objectives we are seeking to understand and achieve:

(1) A clearer recognition that we are spirits functioning through consciousness, and that all our experiences must flow, for good or ill, according to the quality and intensity of our thought processes.

(2) We deepened our sense of awareness and realised that thoughts, when focussed by interest, will evoke much detailed information together with a host of associated ideas which provide even greater knowledge.

(3) Everything becomes more alive according to the intensity of our understanding, and the information we absorb about it. We therefore considered in broad detail the personality as an expression of all our thoughts and past experiences. We are today a *pattern* of consciousness which we ourselves have created through our lives, and which we shall use as a basis for evolving our personalities and our creative projects in the future.

(4) Then we discussed the Law of Love as being the central power which everyone can possess. We recognised that when Love is present it transforms the entire personality into a positive, harmonious and effective being. It influences for good all our thought processes, quickens all our virtues, and directly improves our relationships with people, vocation and environment. It is the creative Law, the power which floods the mind with energy, interest, enthusiasm and positive thinking. It is the secret of concentration.

Now we can proceed, ever keeping in mind this great

Law of Multiplying Good and its all-pervading influence on personality and the functions of the mind.

Let me try to depict this in three simple sketches. Here is the first:

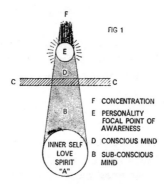

FIG 1

F CONCENTRATION

E PERSONALITY
FOCAL POINT OF
AWARENESS

D CONSCIOUS MIND

B SUB-CONSCIOUS
MIND

INNER SELF
LOVE
SPIRIT
"A"

At the foot (A) we see the inner-self radiating its life through the subconscious mind (B), in which are untold powers and influences. This central power flows through the fluctuating division (C) into the conscious mind (D), which is always the focal point of awareness (E) in every moment.

When our mental faculties are relatively undeveloped, the radiation of our personality is correspondingly weak. And, likewise, its ability to concentrate, select its objective, and create imaginative concepts is diminished. So the power radiating at point (F) is limited.

Consider the second drawing:

Here is the developed mind of a person who is highly educated. A store of knowledge deepens his understanding of the subjects in which he is interested. His imagination is quickened by the constant use of his mind in relation to the way of life which holds his attention.

His personality, therefore, radiates greater power, and

we see at point (F) the increased creative outflow of his interest (love) for the subject to which he gives attention, intense concentration and imagination which will produce corresponding creative results.

This is often the kind of mind we observe in a scientist, business man, politician, surgeon, lawyer, artist and others devoted to intellectual and creative work.

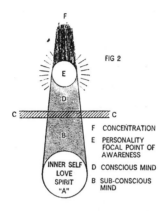

FIG 2

F CONCENTRATION
E PERSONALITY FOCAL POINT OF AWARENESS
D CONSCIOUS MIND
B SUB-CONSCIOUS MIND

In this second illustration you will notice the dividing line (C) between the conscious mind (D), and the subconscious (B) has changed its position. What I am seeking to indicate here is that as we develop and increasingly express our mental abilities, we are thus able to call more and more upon the deep resources of our subconscious.

Thus we become more conscious of the great inborn powers we possess which, naturally, we see evidenced in increased creative ability. Once this is achieved the ability to direct our energies and lives enables us to achieve our desired objectives.

However, one of the dangers of this quickened state of consciousness is that we can become "self-sufficient", thus losing sight of the true spiritual pattern and purpose of our lives.

Now consider the third illustration with extra care, for this is everyman's true potential. In this I endeavour to show the person whose life is centred in all-embracing LOVE. When this is amplified by an awareness of God's Love in *all* things then the spiritual-mental faculties are correspondingly multiplied.

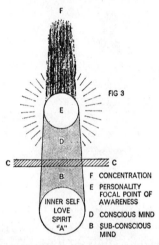

FIG 3

F   CONCENTRATION
E   PERSONALITY
     FOCAL POINT OF
     AWARENESS
D   CONSCIOUS MIND
B   SUB-CONSCIOUS
     MIND

INNER SELF
LOVE
SPIRIT
"A"

The total area of consciousness (D) has increased, and the focal point through which personality ceaselessly expresses itself is greatly augmented (E). Its radiation spreads widely round such a person at all times.

Because Love is the motivating and creative principle the mind concentrates without effort (F). The will to choose and maintain its choice of direction is thus greatly strengthened. And imagination freely paints its pictures of creative projects with the ability to fulfil them.

Whether you are brilliant intellectually or not, in this

THE POWER OF CREATIVE IMAGINATION 71

state of consciousness your life will fulfil its purpose on all levels according to your inborn pattern, for you will then be a balanced spiritual-mental personality of the highest order.

With this high level of consciousness, the intellectual can add greater power to every aspect of his life and work. And every one can awaken to a rich, rewarding and ever deepening experience of this exciting adventure of living.

It is time now to realise the part imagination plays in our mental processes. Interest produces effortless concentration, and sustains our will to choose experience or objective so as to achieve its fulfilment. When love flows through the imagination we have a combination of forces which leads us to final achievement.

Imagination is the faculty you use in every thinking process. Before you initiate any action the mind evokes a picture or a concept of it. Shall we take some simple examples?

A housewife decides (the will) to bake a cake. Her interested mind at once pictures the kitchen oven, the kind of cake she wishes to make and the essential ingredients and actions necessary to produce it. And she has complete faith in both the picture and her ability to bring it into being.

She starts with a precise picture of, say, a birthday cake in her imagination. As she follows this through with sustained thought and resulting actions the cake is made and placed in the oven. Eventually it appears as the desired cake. It is a concrete representation of a mentally conceived objective. No picture—no cake!

A man, with faith in his knowledge and ability, yearns (an aspect of love) to set up his own business. So he ponders and imagines every detail of his project. Perhaps he wants to open a new shop to sell hardware. Long before the shop appears, he spends many hours picturing location, competition, layout, tools, kitchen utensils, refrigerators, nails, screws and a thousand gadgets to meet the needs of the customers he visualises. He imagines staff and financial possibilities and, in fact, constructs the new business in his mind to the best of his ability.

If he persists in his interest and vision, and maintains his faith, he will find that people, events and opportunity unfold. Soon he finds the right property and, step by step, his original vision and desire is finally completed.

Everything that man has ever produced through his personality and inventiveness has followed his imaginative concepts. The house in which you now live, and all it contains, were first pictures in a mind, or minds, involved in constructing it.

Our present civilization in its many forms, every aspect of government, science, industry, electronics, nuclear physics, space travel and world communications, all represent the result of original thoughts first pictured in the imagination. So we see that imagination, linked with love (interest), will power, concentration, memory (knowledge) and faith is vital to the creation of everything that we desire to achieve.

Since my love, interest and enthusiasm is directed towards you, my only purpose is to help *you*. In this present fellowship, the only love-offerings I can contribute are the concepts we are sharing together in the hope that you will take them into your own present and future practical expression.

What, then, would be your ideal objectives? What, within the bounds of reason, would you like to achieve which, when realised, will give you a more satisfying life in your present environment?

Because Love is the Great Law it is always good to set projects which are true to your nature and which will not violate the well-being of anyone. We never accomplish anything worth while if we secure our desires by trampling on others. When we base our concept on Love the power we use is immense, but it carries the grave responsibility of forever advancing the good of our fellows along with any progress we make ourselves.

Let us take for granted your desire to improve your personality and relationships with others. This desire is in the process of unfolding now. Consider carefully the main trends of your life-experience. What gifts have lain dormant, but which you could now bring into effective manifestation? Quite often we never accomplish what is true fulfilment because we see all the various obstacles, and believe it to be impossible. Do have another look at the restrictions and see clearly that if you love the objective enough to visualise it, and persevere steadfastly in your vision and corresponding concentration and action, you will find the way excitingly opening before you. What man can conceive, when he believes and has faith in himself, he can achieve.

If you have a business or vocation, are you happy in it? What would be your vision of greater advancement? Do you want promotion? Then "see" yourself in the new position and dedicate all your interest, thoughts, words and deeds to that end. Motivate your objective through love, expressed as service for all concerned, with *their* well-being always in mind.

If you are a scientist you may be engaged on intensive research and yearn for a "break-through" in your subject. All that we have discussed will quicken this and flow to fill your desire.

Whether housewife or business man, mechanic or doctor, labourer or artist, young or old, you can immediately acquire untold stimulus towards achieving that which is true to your expression. But you must first establish the pattern of it in your mind and keep it alive by constant contemplation, recognition, love, and faith.

The pattern is fundamental, and most of us fail mainly because we abandon or change the pattern which was originally visualised. The mind can produce only what it envisages, and the law of its action is governed by the consistency of the image held before it.

For example: a man creates a vision of a new house, and then all the details are expressed as a plan on paper. Subsequently related ideas, thoughts and actions flow through everyone involved in building it. If the vision and action are maintained then in due course the house appears—a replica of the initial mental vision.

But suppose the planner went round to the house when it was only half completed. He would find a mass of rubble, bricks, cement and scaffolding. If, when contemplating this chaotic scene he lost his interest, frustrated by the apparent difficulties, and abandoned the project, the mental image would immediately be fragmented, and the house would not be finished.

Therefore, when you are considering your own objectives the same principle applies. That is why you should concentrate on those ambitions which you passionately desire to fulfil, and which are so important to you that you will be prepared to maintain a firm application of all your abilities to their accomplishment. There is nothing more stimulating than a major objective for a fully balanced and satisfying life.

What is your ambition today? What can you think of

to capture your main interest? The important question is always—what interests you? No one can interfere with *your* choice! But should you have no particular interest (which is very doubtful) your innermost nature is starved and barren. Wise, indeed, to seek it now!

Much sickness can be alleviated or healed by the same process. Quite apart from spiritual principles, which we shall discuss later, here in the realm of mind the same "image-making" faculty applies. We are quite adept at visualising and executing many material things, and they follow the patterns of our choice. But when we are involved in worry, pain, sickness and other problems the poor mind abandons its own remedial power, and intensifies the pattern of its misfortunes.

Thus we set up in our consciousness the picture our senses are registering. Because it is a painful experience, we accept the pattern of it and then hold it fixed: "I am a sick man," with all the attendant feelings and pain, to support the concept.

The mind tends to maintain that negative attitude which if intense and held long enough, may well sustain or deepen the serious states of disturbance or illness. Trouble, worry, sickness or discordant relationships are nature's way of reminding us of the need to compensate by substituting a vision of the perfect answer. Then, at last, the entire system and events begin to respond in positive ways.

We shall consider this, however, from an infinitely higher point of view later. There are many problems which are too great for most of us to solve ourselves. We shall discuss this in our relationship with God and the power of prayer. But now you are developing a plan for your day linked with immediate and future objectives.

As a keen observer of your own life you will be evaluating the effect of your creative imagination and the flow of your love which quickens it. If you accept this then everyone will be blessed because you have passed their way.

We are now ready to explore another aspect of the mind which represents the eternal spiritual outreach of man. We shall discuss some aspects of the Law of Cause and Effect, but first I hope you will digest all we have talked about.

POWER THOUGHTS

1 Imagination is the creative faculty you use in every thinking process. Everything you have ever achieved was dependent on the "picture" in your mind holding the objective.

2 The imaginative concept was fulfilled according to the degree of your desire (or love) which stimulated your concentrated and consistent application of thought and effort to its fruition. Without a mental "picture" of a task, job or house it would be impossible to bring them into being.

3 Reflect that all creative experience is first and foremost the result of the MIND functioning through love, imagination, will power, faith and concentration.

4 Begin the day with a list of mental objectives. See yourself as a poised and balanced personality expressing goodwill, tolerance, kindness and trust. Decide on the best objectives for the day and know that your thoughts will flow into reality in the right way and at the right time.

5 Get a clear picture of your future objectives. What do you really yearn to achieve? What kind of a person do you want to become? What you can conceive you can achieve. Start now!

THE SHINING PATHWAY

Yea, the darkness hideth not from thee; but the night shineth
as the day; the darkness and the light are both alike to
thee.—PSALM 139: 12.

Let me look out on life with quiet eyes
Seeing God's goodness in the sullen skies,
Glimpsing the shrouded radiance above
The gath'ring clouds that seek to hide His Love.

Though tribulation sore the prospect mars
And mine be but a night of scattered stars,
Yet by their faintly flick'ring rays I see
The glory of a heavenly galaxy.

Now will I fling the casement wide and know
The glittering pathway He would have me go.
Gazing in tranquil faith, where'er I turn
The blazing planets of His brilliance burn.

So will I look on life with trusting eyes,
Scanning in hope serene the midnight skies.
Until in fiery splendour from above
God showers down the meteors of His Love.

"MAC"

Chapter 7

THE LAW OF CAUSE AND EFFECT

I CONTRIBUTE little new knowledge to this discussion with you on the Law of Cause and Effect. We all know and experience it every minute of the day.

I merely mention it, within the context of our present study, to re-focus our attention on this remarkable Law. We are so accustomed to its constant operation that perhaps we seldom pause to think of its mighty action and purpose.

Everything that ever happens to us is the result of some mentally motivated cause. Every action has a corresponding reaction, and this is especially true in the realm of mind.

I write by responding only to mental impulses which direct the flow of words and the physical movements of brain, nerves, body, arm and hand. And so on, through a vast range of action and experience every hour.

Now jog your memory and recall some experiences of the past. Try just for a few moments to recognise the prior mental concepts, decisions and continued concentration and action which produced them. Search for one example of a profoundly good and satisfying episode, and then one which created trouble or disaster. Immediately you are aware of two important events. In one you observe a positive project which created sequences of bliss and creative fulfilment. The other proved to be an error of concept and subsequent motivation which produced a series of events which caused discord, pain or distress. Looking back now with fresh wisdom and an understanding of the hard lesson, you can easily see how you could have planned your way so as to have produced an entirely different result.

I am not suggesting that both these experiences are not equally valuable. I use them simply to illustrate how the mind creates the situations in which we become involved.

It is certain that we are all trying to learn how to live successfully. We are endowed with a relative degree of free-will in that we have the inborn ability to think and choose as we may see fit. We all express our personality between two poles of consciousness—the negative and the positive. Indeed, we would not even be aware of self-consciousness without these essential contrasts.

We cannot know light unless we have darkness by which to contrast it. It is essential to evaluate positive thoughts against negative ones. Like two sides of a coin— they make the whole. We know joy through sadness, happiness through unhappiness, good through evil, well-being through suffering, success through failure, love through hatred, peace through chaos—and so on throughout the full sweep of life in its evolving movement within the negative-positive extremes.

"But," you say, "what about all those things that have burst into my life without either my asking or creating them?" Here, too, if we pause to trace the causes we would recognise the mental motivation of another mind or even many other minds, as in Government, impinging upon your life. At this point, *your* positive reaction will help to determine what will happen next.

Why wars and the many innocents who suffer? Even

now men, women and children somewhere are being killed and maimed through this vile negative disease. Man, through Government, still accepts this way as a means to an end. But the choice is still of mental origin. If the individual has free-will then this is true in the mass through representation. We are all involved equally in every wrong decision by the community in the same way as we are in our own individual choices and reactions.

Children born crippled, insane and diseased? In this world it is often impossible to assess the cause of these tragedies. But with positive compassion for all concerned we can still know, by the very basic laws of creation, that somehow, somewhere, there is a negative cause.

The real reason could stretch back to our forbears, a carry-over of some deeply engrooved upheaval, shock or hereditary taint. Some causes could be due to the all-too evident evils of world conditions—such as atomic radiation, and much wrong thinking. These causes are lost in the intangible. But we can be sure of this: the Law of Cause and Effect is inevitable in its eventual manifestation—whether or not we are able in our lives to assess or discover the full measure of its consequences.

We can, I believe, take comfort and courage from the fact that we are essentially spiritual beings, and that this same Law also produces eternal scope for the positive solution of every situation, without exception. A stricken body is not significant from an eternal point of view, for the moment the spirit is released, as in death, it will stand forth immaculate and perfect to unfold its true nature.

This Law, then, is designed to give us scope for the creative evolution of our personalities and the way of life we choose. It directs, incessantly, our attention to the

creative power of mind and its ability to create negative
or positive experience. Whenever we choose a negative
pattern we always suffer from it in some way. This is
life's way of reminding us to refocus our abilities in a
positive direction and to learn the lesson inherent in the
discord. Whenever we act positively we create satisfying
circumstances. We could all acquire a much greater
peace of mind, and an awareness of the wonderful purpose
of life, could we but understand that every aspect of it is
designed to awaken us to the infinite powers at our
disposal.

The pains and problems, the wars and tragedies, the
worries and fears, the ugly and distressing situations, all
contain the seeds of their ultimate and perfect solution.
They invite our acceptance and spiritual-mental power to
transform them. They are like a block of marble facing a
sculptor. He, in imagination, sees the vision of an angel
imprisoned within it, and proceeds to chip away the
unwanted stone until his angel stands forth supreme and
perfect.

And, of course, we learn about life all along the way.
Every painful experience can be just as great a blessing as
a happy one; for the pain is often the promoter of the joy
round the corner when we "agree with our adversary"
and start creating and implementing positive effects.

It is right, therefore, not to blame the past for present
ills, but rather boldly and joyously, set into operation
all the qualities of love and mind to transform them into
future victories. We learn our biggest lessons from our
mistakes, and discover great faith in our true abilities.

At this point it would be well to remember that we
are closely identified with our bodies as precision instruments which we need to use efficiently. They have, like

any mechanical machine, the need for constant care and attention. We are wise to give out, therefore, a constant flow of love, positive plans, and corresponding actions designed to ensure their well-being. We thus fulfil another aspect of the Law of Cause and Effect when initiating this positive decision which should be linked with exercise, deep breathing, recreation, rest, cleanliness and a balanced diet.

It is not our purpose here to elaborate on this because we all know only too well these basic needs. But if we avoid excess in all its forms and seek a balanced and consistent care for the body we shall be able to function more efficiently for the rest of our lives. At least, that is the body's normal purpose and, granted that it is healthy now, then your way forward is clear. You really know the answers.

The same principle applies if you are sick, for a positive plan and outlook will certainly create the right atmosphere which can, and will, bring about healing and wholeness. We have all met the sick person who dwells on his symptoms and we leave him almost as depressed. But many of us have also met those who have faced illness with a positive fortitude, and this fine quality has been imparted to those around them. A positive reaction is always better than a resigned acceptance of an ill condition.

So I visualise you, an eternal spirit, in control of your life and circumstances, forever directing your personality and expression into positive causes which will produce positive effects.

Now let us consider the significance of the Law of Faith, the Law which probes deep into the heart of the subconscious mind, and beyond that into the Mind of God in Whom we live and move and have our being.

POWER THOUGHTS

1 The Law of Cause and Effect is fundamental to life and to every aspect of the mind and its creative processes. It is the Law within which all creation is expressed.

2 Everything that ever happens to us has its origin in some mentally motivated cause (known or unknown). Every mental expression has a corresponding re-action, or response. All we have ever achieved, or will achieve, must flow into being through this Law.

3 Negative thinking produces negative experience. We can recognise this in much sickness of mind and body, troubles and tribulations, broken homes and unhappiness, the discords of the individual or of nations for they are all the result of the Law of Cause and Effect.

4 Positive thinking, based on love and perfect imagina-tive concepts, expressed in faith and good action, sets into motion powers which produce equivalent good results. These results flow not only into present experience but tend to multiply as time goes on.

5 Recall some action of this Law in your own life for good or ill.

6 Decide how this Law can operate for you today, this week, and in the future.

RECOMPENSE

The desert shall rejoice, and blossom as the rose.

—ISAIAH 35: 1.

God took my fainting soul's most desperate hour
To fashion from its misery a flower.
He drew the curtains of the starless dark,
Waking the feathered rapture of a lark.

God saw my sorrow's dire extremity
And stooped in love to bring forth ecstasy.
Touching the barren soil of my despair
He left a jewelled garden gleaming there.

*   *   *

Out of the sunset, as the hour grows late,
God's golden chariot lingers at my gate.
Hearing the summons of my glad release
I run to meet Him down the paths of peace.
                         "MAC"

Chapter 8

THE LAW OF FAITH

BASICALLY I AM a very simple man; or better, I should say that my highest desire is to become even more humble and concerned only with those truths which are vital to my well-being and that of everyone, everywhere, irrespective of race, colour or creed.

In my active ministry it has been a joyous privilege to meet and mix freely with people of many nationalities. During long missions through the British Isles, Europe, America, Canada, New Zealand, Australia, Africa, India, Ceylon, Greece and other lands, I have gained a clear vision of the equality of all—as people.

Through thousands of consultations with those in sickness, trouble and disrupted relationships a vivid awareness has been born in me of the causes of so much tribulation. And I have observed and assessed the patterns of behaviour which have produced the many varied circumstances.

But one truth has brought me immeasurable joy. The more I have shared fellowship with people, their problems and their hopes, the more I reverence and respect the miracle of their being. It has developed in me a profound faith in mankind, and I marvel at the love, courage, and infinite good that is to be found in everyone without exception.

Certainly I recognise evil and catastrophe, injustice and

ignorance. But, beyond this, in everyone lies the pre-dominant good which is ever revealed in the midst of chaos. Beyond the sin and sickness, ignorance and wrong, are the infinite potentials of multiplying good.

Man is a miracle. I believe in his divinely ordained purpose and have a complete faith in his high and eternal destiny, as an individual and as a whole. It is impossible to discuss the mind and its outreach, its needs and its potential, without taking into consideration this basic truth in relation to mankind. We cannot advance at all without recognition of the equality of all people in the presence of God Who created them.

This fact leaps into importance with greater clarity now than perhaps ever before. Today we can clearly recognise that all the main dangers and disasters in our world have their root causes in lack of love and understanding for people—from one's own personal relationships right through to the international scene.

How to Develop Faith in Yourself

Let us keep this in mind as we try to see what the Law of Faith can tell us. What is it? Like the mind, love, life, eternity—the subject is so vast in potential that it soars beyond human definition. But we really know quite a lot about its action, what it can achieve, and that it is effective on all levels of consciousness—from everyday experiences to illimitable spiritual outreach. Indeed it is a faculty with which we are very familiar. It is that part of our intellect, love and imagination which enables us to accept and believe in things and ideas both within and outside our knowledge. Faith becomes "real" according to the degree and intensity of our acceptance.

Here are some examples. When you stand up and walk

it is because you have faith in your ability to do so. Yet when you were a baby, not strong enough to walk, you saw the giants around you striding about and yearned to do likewise. Your own faith and strength were weak— but eventually through imagination and by practise, failure and success, they developed alongside your increasing control of your body; and soon you, too, could walk, leap and run. From then on you had complete trust in your ability to do these things, for you had Faith.

Most of us would have no faith in our ability to walk along a rope suspended fifty feet above the ground. But others, who yearned to do it, imagined the possibility and cultivated their faith in the project and eventually were able to accomplish this feat with ease. You could walk the same rope now, and with equal ease, if it were lying on the ground! This represents the difference in degree of initial faith between the trained acrobat and you! Simply a question of belief.

You go to work and within the scope of your faith accomplish all which you believe you can do. When asked to take over a more difficult and unfamiliar job you may well doubt your ability, believing it to be beyond your mental or physical capabilities. Alternatively you could accept the new responsibility and, because of your faith in yourself, make a complete success of it.

The scene confronting you now—whether room, office, street or countryside—is "real" to you, according to your interpretation because you accept and believe in your presence and in the reality of the environment. Thus a vast and ever-changing sequence of accomplishments and experiences demonstrate their reality within the framework of your recognition and belief. We could not live

as free-will personalities without this basic faith in ourselves and our own interpretation of other people and
environment. Furthermore, we could never embark on
any new project without faith in our ability to accomplish
it.

We have discussed at this point many aspects of personality and facets of love, intellect, memory, will power and
imagination; now we can see that they are all dependent
on our Faith, or belief, or recognition, of their powers
and potentials in expression. It has been said, "What
man can conceive, he can achieve." Yes—but only if
he has faith in his idea, faith in himself and the consistent
application of his abilities to bring the conception into
being.

Because we are talking together and united in exploring
the latent powers of personality my main interest is *you*,
all that you are, and all that you can become. Even
though to establish this contact with you I am writing
these thoughts in my motor-caravan in the countryside,
I am still aware of your presence. I have faith that the
ideas I seek to share will reach all those who can benefit
by them. My faith, quickened by love and imagination,
has already created a way through to you. So although
this is only a mental picture linked with faith, the fact
that you are now reading these words represents the
reality and fulfilment of my vision.

Our communion, therefore, is as realistic as if you were
sitting by me now. My faith was, in our relationship, the
reality held in mind, subsequently achieved by our
meeting each other in consciousness.

What, then, is *your* faith? It would be a thrilling
event for me to hear you tell of all the qualities of your
mind and experiences in which you have complete trust.

As you cannot do this, why not spend some time contemplating these precious gifts? You could even write them down for your own appreciation.

What gifts of intellect and way of life do you best express? Do you have complete faith in your ability to fulfil the work or interests in which you are engaged? Can you believe in your ability to fulfil whatever plan you formulate for specific objectives? What do you most want to do? Are you able to kindle faith in yourself to achieve it?

You should examine all your present qualities and desires for the future in relation to what we have discussed, and to seek a more vigorous appreciation of yourself and your potentials. The law of life is that you must cultivate faith in yourself and your destiny as an eternal being passing through this world. Learn how to use your mind in the highest and most creative way.

How to Strengthen Your Faith in God

Seeking to keep our discussion as simple as possible, we have talked so far about many fascinating aspects of our personal nature. We have explored some of the essentials and pointed to much that we can accomplish through our own abilities sharpened by positive thinking.

But it is not enough just to seek a personal evaluation. We are also involved in the world and are linked with three thousand million other people who, like ourselves, are living on this small globe and hurtling endlessly through space and time round the sun.

What about the earth itself? All round us we see the incredible spectacle of nature, the exuberant growth of vegetation and countless forms of life. The sun quickens all creation on the planet. The seasons come and go.

New children arrive and adults depart in an endless procession. We thrill at the beauty of a sunset, the grandeur of mountains, lakes and dales. A flower in a garden can move us to tears, and a field of corn holds promise of a rich harvest.

No need for me to tell you about the wonder of it all. By the Grace and Purpose of an Unseen Power you have been given life, and have always been aware of your physical environment. Our purpose now is to clear our minds of any uncertainties which may exist about our faith in God, the supreme Intelligence and Presence Who has brought it all into being.

Living as we do in the tiny speck of mind, engrossed in our own affairs and difficulties, we often lose sight of our own involvement in all of life and the plan of a Divine Creation.

Man, the thinker and seeker, has always held the idea of God as Creator and Arbiter of his destiny. But man has also evolved a number of differing ideas about Him, and how to commune with Him. The present religious scene is so complicated that many find great difficulty in knowing what to believe, or what teaching to follow. It is quite beyond me to find a way through the incredible labyrinths of religion though I believe, completely, in the main stream of love, faith and prayer. But for our purpose now let us try to recognise a valid and *realistic* reason why we should have a complete and abiding faith in God.

As we have seen, everything we experience is motivated and governed by our invisible mind processes. And we watch elusive ideas producing physical effects. When we consider man himself we pass beyond argument directly we realise that, whatever else, such a mechanism as life, mind and body could never come into being without a

THE LAW OF FAITH

Mind great enough to conceive and create it. A baby, from seed to its appearance in the world, could never be formed by accident or a haphazard chemical mixing of ingredients.

This truth equally applies to any form of nature, from the neutrons and electrons of atoms to the ordered patterns of stones, soil, vegetation, insects and animals. The observable system of all that is created in the world tells us of the Planning and Production of an Almighty Thinker. There cannot be a universe of law and mathematical order without the Law-maker.

We behold, not the invisible Presence, but the outward products of that Presence. The world, all life, and the universe in the illimitable depths of space proclaim the Omnipresence and Omnipotence of God.

Most of us suffer from a sense of separation from the whole, induced, of course, by our intense sense of personal being as a separate entity. But, in truth, we are part of the Whole, of Everything. Indeed, we must be part of the Being of God as an Omnipresent Reality. Yet it is also true that, because one of our greatest gifts is free-will, we can exist in our own right, accept any idea or belief, and reject or recognise God as we choose.

As we evolve slowly in wisdom and awareness of the greater realities of life and its purposes we inevitably become more able to accept the truth that in the midst of self-awareness we awaken to God-awareness. But for the moment let us define creation and life as existing within the One Mind of God—the Power which creates and maintains everything in orderly and evolving patterns. Since we, too, are minds, it should not be impossible to conceive a communion with the God-Mind of Almighty Power and Purpose.

I suggest the first step upward in faith is the recognition of our unity with the whole, and our unity with the Presence of God based on the evidence of our own being and the world in which we live. From that focal point we can move forward to a consideration of specific methods and means whereby communion with God and the experience of Divine influences can be cultivated and experienced.

All round us is evidence of God's work in creation. Pause for a moment and think what our lives would be like if, using our free-will, faith and imagination, we could accept that the same God is ever seeking to implement His Perfect Plan through each one of us thereby revealing His Purpose for creating us. In the light of such a simple, basic Christian truth, it is breath-taking to turn to the life and teaching of Jesus Christ as found in the New Testament, and there find clear confirmation, not only of the truths we have already discussed, but also full instructions how they can be all accomplished in infinitely greater ways through love, faith and prayer—based on communion with God.

It is revealing and remarkable that in our age of great intellect and knowledge, just when many have begun to think they are self-sufficient in their own technical ability, we are being swept into an appreciation of our urgent need to embrace spiritual values to ensure the safety, sanity and progressive well-being of mankind.

Beyond the many varied confusing attitudes of Christianity, evolved by man through the centuries, we witness the inviolable truths which, when recognised and implemented, are vested in every church of all denominations. When we become totally centred in faith, love and prayer, in utter simplicity, tolerance and equality, then the "Signs and Wonders" will flow into our lives.

Beyond the Christian faith is the rest of humanity and its beliefs. In this enlightened age it would be irreconcilable with reason to suggest that God made a mistake when He created people of different races, colours, and of different philosophies. Surely there is only one Father of all mankind? And surely He must offer the same indivisible Love and purpose and ultimate eternal freedom to all?

It is not my purpose here, however, to discuss the merits of the many religions but rather to concentrate on what Christianity has to offer. For here, at last, we have the perfect pattern which, could we but follow it, would transform us all.

All that we have discussed leads us to this high point of faith in ourselves, faith in our fellows, and faith in God, linking our lives with His in Love through Jesus Christ. Because all the teaching of Jesus is based on love for God and love for people, we have a truth which is not only practical but of tremendous potency. As Christians, if I may so label ourselves, this is our first responsibility in faith. Without love we are nothing.

If we desire to advance in our experience of faith and prayer we shall never make much headway without the Love which is God. This involves an abandonment of all prejudice, intolerance, injustice and judgment of others. Let each of us worship, believe and express in complete freedom—but let our own lives be founded on absolute respect for, and friendship towards, every other man. Then we can have *one Church of Christ* in the hearts of all people, demonstrated in many ways through numerous denominations.

I direct your mind to this because I believe the Christian

D

has a very special privilege, responsibility and opportunity to create bridgeheads of understanding across every human dilemma and difference. The only true objective for any Christian is the complete brotherhood of man in the Fatherhood of God. Then, indeed, the world will marvel at the reality of Christ.

It is not my purpose to dwell on the Christian gospels. You know them already. I merely emphasise their basic reality, and want to encourage you to accept and to experience fully the astonishing transformation that follows the concept of, and belief in, the powers of love, faith and prayer. These are necessarily personal and intimate experiences. No other person can do your loving for you. No-one can exercise your faith, and it is your singular privilege to pray. I can bear witness only through my own experience that in this direction lies the real potential and infinite extension of the individual and mankind. Later we shall consider some examples of answered prayer in which complete transformations and healings took place. You will discover that the results were beyond the skill of mere man.

Now I wish to point to the deep awareness of human consciousness that is sweeping across the world. Today there are hundreds of stories reporting the findings of the modern pioneers who have seriously experimented and recorded their findings in the power of Christian Prayer. They all report the same experience—that when complete love for God and for people is implemented, and faith founded on the Almighty Presence as Perfection in the midst of chaos, there is a Divine response. There are thousands of case histories which tell of these remarkable events. They read like the miracles of the gospels and the early Church. These testimonies are significant, not only from the point of view of physical healing, but also in relation to the outreach and progress of mankind.

We should evaluate this significance in terms of new and infinite dimensions of consciousness and creativeness. It poses no less a question than: what kind of life would we be expressing if all the knowledge, wisdom, love and power of God were freely manifested in our daily experience? This is what prayer potentially offers—according to our faith and concept.

There are, as you can see, abundant reasons for your own personal faith in yourself, in people and in God.

Finally, therefore, what *do* you believe? Can you accept these basic truths and apply them to your own present experience and to your own denominational religious allegiance? Can you see some aspects of personality, or plans for the future which can be augmented by your faith?

It is certainly worth while, in quiet moments, to contemplate your own faith and to assess it in relation to everyday happenings. In fact, now that we have progressed thus far in our search it would help you to keep all these ideas alive by re-reading them.

We began with such a vast subject that we could only glimpse the main themes. But as you re-read the various points your own awareness will deepen and you will see how they can be related to your needs and objectives.

From this point we shall go on to discuss many other aspects of our spiritual qualities. But before exploring the deep significance of prayer, I should like to talk a little more about people and their environment; and as prayer often involves our attitudes to health I think we should also discuss prayer in relation to medical science. But first may I say that as we are now going to talk about spiritual matters, in no way do I seek to persuade you to violate your cherished convictions. Far too much harm has been done by trespassing on, and intolerance towards, the spiritual views of others. My only concern is for you, for I have a deep feeling of reverence for your life and all that you are. I respect and am thankful for this opportunity to walk with you in the precious and beautiful garden of your mind. But I would not crush or destroy any one of the blooms you have grown there. Rather will I, as a brother, share with you and help you.

If there is one paragraph in this book which helps you, then I am grateful. The rule I apply to myself is an absolute respect for the life and work of others. If I read, then, with an open mind, I will find *that which is true for me* and leave that which is not. But my tolerance and respect remain, for if I condemn a whole work because some ideas do not concur with my own, I might miss the jewel that belonged to me.

Let God bless you in your reading, for, in the end, that is the only truth of enduring significance.

As (a man) thinketh in his heart, so is he. Prov. 23:7.

*　　*　　*

Before going on to the next chapter may I share with you a true story of how love, faith and prayer brought great Blessings to a family?

I had been travelling on a mission through the United States and Canada, and eventually came to Victoria, in British Columbia. After a service in the Metropolitan United Church, I was invited to the home of this family. Prompted by one of her friends the mother told me, simply, about a child who was healed through love, faith and prayer.

Although she and her husband had children of their own, there came a time when they yearned to adopt another child. So they asked the Lord to send them the right one. Eventually they were offered a little girl—a pathetic child with dislocated hips and a "squeezed" and twisted face.

They prayed together and then, with the unmistakable inward awareness, they just *knew* this was the baby the Father had chosen for them. They felt great compassion for this little one and her plight, and then gladly accepted her as God's Gift.

Being a family of love and believing in the promises of Jesus Christ to heal, they simply offered themselves to Him for the healing of the child's distorted hips and face. Day by day, week by week and month by month, they steadfastly cherished her and gave thanks to God for His Perfection filling this little life. And they saw complete restoration taking place.

The hips became strong and perfect, and the face no longer distorted. The Lord worked through them, the doctors, and the prayer group. At last all was well. I saw the young girl myself, then seven years old, normal and beautiful.

I marvelled while listening to this miracle of God's Love, and to the confirmation by members of the Church Prayer Group who were visiting with me. Yes—Christ's Love *is* marvellous, for in the Christian churches we see so many lives mended by it. And yet the mother was quite unconscious of her own Christ-like dedication and faith which made the healing possible.

It is, of course, not unusual for people to have love enough to adopt a child, and we can all thank God that so many children find sanctuary in this way. But most of us would probably be very careful in assessing the responsibilities inherent in our choice. It is one thing to accept a happy, healthy, cuddly little child—and quite another to take one who might grow up to be a cripple, unable to walk!

To this Canadian family the Lord had said, "I would like you to adopt this one." And through obedience and trust the broken body was healed. His Love filled them all with joy and strength.

We can all come into God's Presence when praying with a child in our arms. It is as though a door opens to reveal new and tender dimensions of love, peace, joy and power which are often beyond our adult ability to reach. Or, perhaps, it is that when we pray in these circumstances the accumulated scars of sin, suffering and worldly cares dissolve as we stand face to face with the Lord, Whose love is shining through the little one. "For of such is the Kingdom of God."

I am sure you must have been blessed through children in this way. Perhaps it may be your privilege to help others who are anxious about their children, and to clear away their doubts by bringing them to the Lord in love and prayer.

Thank You, Father, for lifting us into Your Love for all Your children so that the new generation will really be known as the sons of God on earth, through Jesus Christ, our Lord.

Power Thoughts

1 Faith in yourself is basic to every expression of love, imagination, will-power and concentration to achieve every goal—great or small.

2 Faith in God is as natural and simple as our faith in our being, and the reality of the world in which we live. We exist, beyond all speculation or argument, in a universe of planned creation which functions through Higher Laws. We observe in man and nature the power and the product of Infinite Intelligence forever indwelling and motivating everything.

3 Embrace, with total acceptance, this ultimate truth about yourself and your relationship with God. Know that you are moving into new dimensions of consciousness which are linked with the creative Power-thinking of God—infinite and multiplying GOOD.

4 Consider the amount of faith you have in yourself and your way of life. Venture into the work of this day believing in your gifts, and that you will leave a creative mark on everything you do, and on every person you meet.

5 Let go worry about the tasks which confront you. Believe that the Power of God is with you in all your undertakings, and be aware of the increasing good you will encounter.

PART OF THE WHOLE

And God said, Let us make man in our image, after our likeness.—GENESIS 1: 26.

> *I am a part of God, Who is the Whole;*
> *One with the mountain and the forest tree;*
> *Sunrise and sunset centre in my soul*
> *And every flow'r that blooms hath birth in me.*

I am the eagle soaring in the height,
The sparkling rivulet, the sylvan glade,
Gladness of dawning, sacred peace of night,
The star-strewn heavens and the woodland shade.

I am the immortal promise of the Spring,
The flame of Autumn burns within my breast;
Mine is the harmony the Summers sing,
The Winter purity of snow-clad rest.

I am a part of all created things,
And He Who fashioned them hath made me too.
Lord, Who hast given to my spirit wings
Bid me ascend and lose myself in You.

"MAC"

Chapter 9

PRAYER AND MEDICAL HEALING

As you will have realised, the essential purpose of our talks is to form a concept of the powers we all possess, and to use them in a balanced way which does not interfere with the beliefs and customs of others. As I have emphasised, Love is the essential quality for the well-being and progress of everyone. The inherent gifts of mankind are to think, imagine, have faith, pray, and express personality as best he can. But here we are confining ourselves to those qualities which can open for us a richer and fuller way of life where we are.

The moment we consider the possibility of answered prayer the entire field of well-being and physical healing comes into perspective. Yet we are wise to consider this in relation to the great research, knowledge and skills that the medical profession has developed to help the sick.

When some great discovery is made there is often a temptation to isolate it and proclaim the new way as exclusive to those who practise it. Although many people have been healed through spiritual principles and prayer, this does not justify the abandonment of all that man has discovered in his own right. God works through all mankind, and not least through doctors, nurses and others who minister to those who are ill. But before we discuss this in some detail, let me quote the experience and vision of some eminent doctors.

Many in the medical world know Dr. Alexis Carrel, Member of the Rockefeller Institute, Nobel Prize 1912, winner of the Nordhoff-Jung Medal for cancer research. Thousands of people have read his famous work *Man the Unknown*. Here a world-famous doctor repeats just what Jesus and His followers have been saying for centuries. He endorses the experience of all who work in the Ministry of Divine Healing, and I have come to the same conclusion in my own work. He emphasises the mental causes of disease, and the need to release them spiritually. He writes:

"Thought can generate organic lesions. The instability of modern life, the ceaseless agitation, create states of consciousness which bring about nervous and organic disorders of the stomach and of the intestines, defective nutrition and the passage of intestinal microbes into the circulatory apparatus. Various kidney and bladder infections are the remote results of mental and moral imbalance. Such diseases are almost unknown in social groups where life is simpler, where anxiety is less constant. Likewise, those who keep the peace of their inner self in the midst of tumult are immune from nervous and organic disorders."[1]

Again in his little book *Prayer*, Dr. Alexis Carrel tells us:

"Prayer has sometimes, so to speak, an explosive effect. Patients have been cured almost instantaneously of afflictions such as lupus of the face, cancer, kidney troubles, ulcers, tuberculosis of the lungs, of the bones or peritoneum. The phenomenon is produced nearly always in the same way. Great pain, then the feeling of being cured.

[1] *Man The Unknown* by Dr. Alexis Carrel is published in England by Hamish Hamilton Limited of London by whose kind permission this extract has been used.

In a few seconds, at most a few hours, the symptoms disappear and the anatomic lesions mend. The miracle is characterised by extreme acceleration of the normal processes of healing. Never has such an acceleration been observed up till now in the course of their experiences by surgeons and physiologists. . . . Such are the results of prayer of which I have a sure knowledge . . . this mass of phenomena introduces us into a new world, the exploration of which has not begun and which will be fertile in surprises. What we already know for certain is that prayer produces tangible effects. However strange this may appear, we must consider as true, that whosoever asks receives, and that the door is opened to him who knocks."[1]

When a man of Dr. Carrel's stature and experience as a surgeon, doctor and physiologist, endorsed by his laboratory research on the regeneration of tissues and the healing of wounds, makes such statements, the wise will appreciate the significance of them.

Among the speakers at a Conference of the Scottish Healing Fellowship was Dr. Ernest Claxton, Principal Assistant Secretary to the British Medical Association.

The following summary of his address comes from *For Health and Healing*, published by the Guild of Health, by whose permission this summary is used. It is most impressive that such statements should be made by a medical man of such high standing.

Dr. Claxton began by saying that it is necessary to find meaning in life. The Fall of Man was basic in human society. Disharmony had occurred somewhere, and since then there had been a struggle to recreate harmony. Salvation is health, the transference from being fallen to

[1]*Prayer* by Dr. Alexis Carrel is published in England by Hodder and Stoughton of London by whose kind permission this extract has been used.

being redeemed. Do we allow the process of healing to
go on in us? We must look at it in detail, in relation to
sick people and to society.

The Healing Spirit emerges at many points in life. Dr.
Claxton used the analogy of the power of water in a
water-pistol, and compared it with that in Niagara Falls
—we must not forget that every facet of healing is part of
something greater. Healing is the restoration of function
and shape in the individual, and there is a great healing
process to restore harmony in the cosmos—unity between
God and man. We believe it happens through Calvary, self
giving co-operation with God's will, resulting in redemp-
tion. We can apply this process and be part of it in every
sphere.

Healing is a sign of life—dead things don't heal. A
stone can't heal, but a bone can. If we have life in us, we
can heal or be healed. There are two kinds of life—(1)
Physical life which we were given at birth and (2) Rebirth.
The reborn individual has a greater healing capacity for
himself and for others. There is a tendency to heal in any
case if a being is alive. Faith is important, and the same
power is available for the individual and for society as a
whole. He referred to the Apostles' Creed where the Holy
Catholic Church is mentioned, saying that the Healing
Spirit operates more strongly through a fellowship than by
means of an individual.

An experience of Jesus Christ makes our body different,
we can have life everlasting, which is life without limitations. In Christ, there is life going on beyond death
and this begins and happens now. One can be imprisoned
in a house, or by paralysis, or one can be free. All disability is due to sin—one's own or someone else's. If
something is wrong, the Spiritual Law has been broken

somewhere—it may be due to some incident in childhood which does not mature for many years. Even stupidity may be a sin. We must strive for a society where these things don't happen. In proportion to our obedience, we attain the joy of the Healing Spirit, curing and resolving sin. Getting better for its own sake is quite inadequate, with a big selfish element in it. If self-preservation is not related to a greater plan, it is a selfish thing.

The Healing Spirit goes on automatically and can be aided by human agency, such as medicine, an operation, and the like, so that the power can work better. Are we seeking healing of the disease or of the person? A healed personality may have a diseased or deformed body, but the healing occurs much better if the person becomes reborn. There may be freedom from symptoms as the inherited life within is reinforced by rebirth. Illnesses will disappear after a change of heart where there is not organic destruction, though we believe this too can be made good. The environment is important—if it is God-centred, it enables the individual to come to terms with God and with himself. It is also easier to get better if there is a purpose, such as to be fully able to co-operate with God. If the illness is used as part of that, it is no longer to be resented, and therefore gets better more quickly.

Prayer, Laying on of Hands, and the Sacraments can all be used. Let us take what intelligent action we can and not limit prayer to the individual, but also use it for the sick society. We must apply the power of God to any disability of body, mind or heart.

The effect of the Holy Spirit is shown by our caring, so that we will go to no end of trouble. If we can't stand someone, there is a complete block to the Holy Spirit. We need to find from God the power to care for people. Satan creates a divisive spirit.

Some people have a charismatic gift (healing power), sympathy, love, power in Laying on of Hands. We all have it to some extent. A sympathetic doctor may express it in the way in which he handles the patient.

With regard to society, political reforms may be necessary, but something deeper is needed. It is important to have right relationships with people and with God. There are practical rules. In our family life, we must not keep up quarrels, but must be willing to accept blame honestly when necessary, and achieve forgiveness of ourselves and the other person. We must have the courage to be different and to unite with people of other classes, colour, age or religious denominations. Within the churches there should be a common purpose, with differences dissolved and the churches on fire and fighting to influence and change people. Relationships can be resolved by this common purpose.

Reborn individuals can deal with world-hunger, population-control, housing or industrial problems, and so on. We must have rebirth and renewal of our own spirit, believing that God has a plan for everyone. If we are fully given to God, we shall be conformed to the image of His Son.

Dr. Claxton went on to speak of depression, which he said was a sin. Most mental illness is due to self-concern. It can be helped by caring, by drugs and if the patient is given an interest, i.e. practical action by other people. Some people cannot pull themselves together, but others can. There must be love, patience and care. Peace of mind, courage, serenity and closeness to God must be fostered.

He also touched on the question of unanswered prayer, and said that some prayers should never have been prayed.

The Prayer of Faith should be preceded by the Prayer for Guidance.

Dr. Claxton ended by asking for prayers for the medical profession, that they may be able to teach people to live in such a way that they may not become ill.

Confirmation comes from yet another eminent medical man. When Sir Sydney Alfred Smith, Professor of Forensic Medicine at Edinburgh University, was addressing a doctors' graduation ceremony, he clearly pointed the way into the future.

He said that much of the future in preventive medicine lay in obtaining clearer knowledge of the relationship between mind and body, and how their functions were controlled and harmonised.

He urged doctors to do more to understand the nature of cures by prayer and faith, which would give them insight into "this uncharted territory of medicine," with its entirely new vistas in the maintenance of health through early diagnosis and adjustment of disturbances which probably occurred long before disease made itself manifest. He said:

"The importance of balanced action in all the processes of the body, mind and spirit, has been noted by scientists and philosophers over the past 5,000 years, but it now rests with us—it rests with you doctors—to bring it into the field of medical teaching and practice. This question has already intruded violently into the field of medical treatment, and we must encourage and stimulate research on these relationships. . . ."

He pointed out that there were few doctors who could not recall instances in which prayer or faith had brought about a dramatic change in some seemingly hopeless case. . . . "We should do much more to try to understand the nature of such phenomena."

Here is light indeed, a sign of the times, coming from so famous a source as the Faculty of Medicine in Edinburgh.

We are truly blessed that new vision is opening the way to infinite possibilities. Even as doctors begin to see the significance of psychological research, so now both psychologist and doctor must lift their vision to the implication of spiritual principles and the power of prayer.

We should envisage the significance of all our spiritual qualities, and prayer, together with a deeper understanding of the medical skills which can be deployed in every need. When both doctor and patient establish a partnership which embraces spiritual, psychological and physical needs we shall be on the high road to a quicker and more enduring healing of mind and body.

Vision for Medical Science

In his many fields of specialised knowledge the doctor is an efficient partner with nature in the healing process. But what is nature?

The slashed finger, cleansed, stitched and protected from infection by the doctor, proceeds to heal by astonishing natural processes which build new cells and release many curative and protective agents to the area of the wound. The human agent straightens and links a broken bone, but nature seals it with new bone tissue. In brilliant surgical operations, the surgeon removes diseased tissues, and works on the heart, liver, stomach, brain and, indeed, every part of the body. He observes some malfunction and in the light of vast research and knowledge seeks to rearrange the system, thus enabling it to resume its normal functions.

Whatever the doctor does within the limits of his knowledge and skill he finds the natural healing process co-operating with him to complete it. But, with the psychologist, he also knows with ever-growing understanding that the body is closely identified with the life-force and with the mind. Just as he knows that bodily pain disturbs consciousness, so does he know that the mind also directly influences, for good or ill, the physical functions.

Every family doctor knows that to the extent he is able to establish a comforting and faith-stimulating relationship with the patient, he is automatically quickening and safeguarding the healing process.

In serious cases, if the patient loses the will to live, the healing power is greatly reduced and medical aid may well fail. A serious sickness so often becomes healed when the patient is poised in peace, is confident of the outcome and has faith in his doctors and nurses.

More and more attention is being paid to detailed assessment of mental-emotional states and their direct relationship to physical disorders. The doctor's purpose should be to clear away the personal worries and fears which do delay healing. Every doctor and psychiatrist now know that there may be intense stresses of the mind which are *causing* the physical disturbance. The medical dictum in healing is not only to clear the outward condition, but also to remove the cause as far as it can be discovered.

The psychiatrist excels in this field. He is the doctor of the mind, working on mental-emotional disturbances. Not only does he perceive the disruptive effect of inward compulsions, stresses and strains, and the dangers of broken relationships in nervous or mental breakdowns, but he can also often relate these states to physical ills.

There is, as I have said, an increasing recognition of this mind-body relationship, and a growing partnership between doctor and psychologist.

But there is a third factor which is often neglected: relatively few doctors or psychologists have much to say with authority about the *spiritual nature* of the patient. Yet here is the root of so many mental and physical troubles. Fear, worry, tension, frustration, bitterness and all disturbed relationships are essentially spiritual problems, and so much could be done to solve them by doctor and patient recognising this truth.

Doctors, of course, hesitate to plough into the ramifications and complexities of religion. But, surely, when we go beyond denominational concern and seek to recognise the basic spiritual needs, we can establish an authoritative vision that is focussed on the total healing of the spirit, mind and body of a broken life?

Does this not, at least, open the way to a wider partnership between ministers and doctors in their respective spheres? What a powerful new dispensation would come about if the doctors announced with authority the need for spiritual re-adjustment, and advised their patients to contact ministers whom they knew to be proficient in spiritual counselling!

It is inevitable that some such recognition and practice will come into being. It is the highway forward, in research and progress, to the creation of the whole man.

In the light of all the present research into the depth and significance of spiritual principles and prayer, and the finding of so many spiritual-mental-emotional causes of human sickness and distress, we should all recognise that the prevention of much disease lies in this new direction.

A balanced personality, centred in love, secure in faith,

poised in peace and positive thinking, is much less likely to become sick. Such a personality is functioning at the highest mental-emotional level, and the healthy mind will not be disturbing the metabolism and harmonious action of the physical system. Surely it is better to prevent than to cure!

The doctor cannot afford to ignore the importance of prayer. He, like the minister, is passionately devoted to helping those in trouble. Both are working on common ground for the healing of the sick. And many ministers have had remarkable experiences of mental and physical transformations following prayers of love and faith. Too many people have been healed in this way for this power-force to be condemned or ignored. So many authenticated case histories of Divine healing have been reported that it seems absurd that human reason and intelligence should not explore and implement this spiritual force which, if not new, is ignored by so many.

As I have said earlier in this book, we all concentrate on the subject which holds our attention. It is the same with healing but the majority of doctors, deeply involved, carry out their arduous duties along conservative and established ways.

It is the same with many ministers who confine themselves to spiritual matters involving faith and prayer. As with doctors, they have little time for looking beyond their immediate duties.

This creates a void, or at best a very flimsy bridgehead, between the two parties. But, when the all-embracing truth is known, neither can really afford this semi-isolation when lives are at stake. The interest of minister and doctor is fundamentally the same, so true partnership should be natural, only waiting fulfilment.

Perhaps, unconsciously, much harm has been done to the cause of Divine healing by the more ardent supporters claiming their method to be the exclusive and best way. But this attitude may have been provoked by the unco-operative attitude of the medical profession.

I firmly believe that God works through all people, and especially through those who seek to serve others. This gives me a profound respect for all who serve in the medical profession, and equally for those who seek healing through prayer and every other spiritual means.

I can see both methods as being potentially magnified in power by a complete recognition of this truth, leading to an all-embracing partnership between doctor, minister and patient. Spirit, mind and body on this earth are indivisible, and the well-being of the whole nature of man is our true objective.

Vision for the Patient

So much of our discussion is particularly applicable to you, if you are sick now, or should be in the future. There is no need to repeat all the principles outlined. So let us now concentrate on specific attitudes to adopt when troubles or sickness come upon you.

You will, as suggested, examine the various aspects of your life, and initiate any corrective action as far as your understanding and ability enable you to do so. Consult your doctor about the symptoms which are disturbing you. And from that moment give him, and everyone who is helping you, in hospital or at home, your absolute trust. Recognise that God works through the doctor, surgeon or nurse, that He is guiding them in their good work, and that He is also filling you with His healing power now!

Pray with simple faith, and wholly accept God's peace,

power and presence. Understand once more you are an eternal spirit and that your mind is receptive to all God's Blessings which protect, enfold and manifest in every way for your highest good. Consult your minister, prayer group, or whoever you choose, to pray with you and for you. Release the burden to God through them. Others can pray perhaps more positively than you because they are not befogged by your condition. But remember always the blind beggar who called to Jesus for help and was healed.

With simple trust and courage, feel free from the pressure of carrying your burdens alone. Turn your attention to others, as far as you can, to love, bless, help and encourage them in every way. From your standpoint this is similar to the ideal minister-doctor-patient relationship, and wonderful things will be in the making as you persevere with it. I remember the healing of Mrs. D. Carrington, who lives at 6 Hallwood Avenue, Salford 6, Lancs. This is just what happened to her, told in her own words, when there was spiritual co-operation between her and us in our Sanctuary, and with the work of the doctors and nurses. Here is her story:

"I had had colitis for eighteen months. I then went to hospital for an examination and was told that I had a malignant growth and ulcers in the bowel.

"I was operated on. Following my operation I had a period of four months convalescence. During this time further tests were made and X-rays taken, and I was advised that another operation would be necessary. It was at this point that I heard about the work of Brother Mandus. This was towards the end of September, 1959.

"My very good friend, Mr. Yates, the minister of the Congregational Church in Irlam o'th'Heights, wrote to Brother Mandus asking him to join in prayer for me.

"By 9th November I was back in the hospital again. This time it was for the removal of the lower bowel. But by 9th December I was home. The surgeon had found it impossible to perform the necessary operation because of the effects of another operation which had taken place way back in 1939. I was therefore sent home as incurable, and my husband was told that I would live for perhaps eighteen months to two years. He was also told that I could not be expected to live any longer than this because these internal growths would eventually close the bowel completely.

"An appointment was made for me to see you, Brother Mandus; but, if you remember, you were called out of town and had to give me a fresh appointment. This second appointment also fell through because Mr. Yates, our minister, who was to take me in his car to the Sanctuary, suddenly fell ill.

"I felt very, very strongly that this was God's way of working because in my true self I felt really afraid to go to the Sanctuary at that time. I didn't want to go to any Divine healing services either, or even to be seen in public at all. I just didn't want to be bothered. Even when Mr. Yates came and showed me that first letter he had from you cancelling the appointment and giving me a fresh one, I told him I was glad.

"Then in May 1960 you came to Cadishead to take a Divine healing service. Nothing could now keep me back. I was really ready—I was! My hubby, Mr. Yates and myself all went along. You talked about love and of loving one another. You asked the people who needed help to stand up, and prayed with one half of the church at a time.

"We began to pray for the sick on the side of the church opposite to where I was sitting. While you were praying for those people, I really was loving them just as you told us to, and I felt that it didn't matter about me any more so long as they were healed. That was just how I felt.

"Eventually you came to me and asked what the trouble was, and whether I believed that God could cure me. I said, 'Yes, I do.' You said, 'Be you healed. Be you perfect as He is perfect.' That is all you said. Those were the exact words. You didn't put your hands on me at all, but I felt a hand placed on my shoulder, ever so lightly, and peace flowed all through me. Then all inside me I felt warm and aglow. It wasn't your hand, Brother Mandus, because I was told that you never touched me, so I know that it was God Who laid His hand on me.

"I wanted to shout for joy, 'I am cured'—I often wonder what would have happened if I had done so. Anyway, I didn't shout because of the beautiful quietness. I knew I was cured because all the pain went and I could sit down without having to sit on my air-ring, and the bleeding had ceased.

"I now felt I wanted to tell everyone what God could do for them, so I started to visit all the sick people who needed help, comfort, courage and faith. I was actually asked to go and see many people I had never known before. Isn't it wonderful how God works?

"Then my hubby bought me a tape-recorder. We got some of your tapes and used a child's push-chair to take our tape-recorder round on our visits.

"The wonderful specialist and surgeon in my hospital was so thrilled with the Divine healing which he knew had taken place. I went to him for many further examinations. I went to him at first every two months, then every three months, and now every six months. I will always remember his gentle encouragement and happiness for me, and his saying to me, 'God has done for you what I couldn't. Keep it up!' What a great work God is doing all the time through him.

"I kept right on visiting and praying for the sick and in June 1961, after a visit to the Sanctuary, I had a vision of having a little healing Sanctuary in our church at Irlam o'th'Heights. It was to be a place where people could come specially for Divine healing. Mr. Yates and I, and lots of my new friends and wonderful old friends, worked on this.

"On June 19th, 1962, the new Sanctuary in our church was consecrated. We are always busy, and so happy with our prayer meetings and visits to the sick. We do see such wonderful results.

"This story goes on and to me every day is a Holy day. I just want to say a special 'Thank you' to my husband, Harold. I couldn't have got through without him. He is a pillar of strength and encouragement and I love him —I do. His work takes him into the homes of lots and lots of people, and he has shared this story with many people in need. Many of these people we have visited together, prayed for and seen get better.

"What can I say? THANK YOU, FATHER."

*   *   *

All things are possible with God when we loosen our bonds and prejudices, and unite on all levels to allow the Father to bring His power to bear.

Now we are ready to cover some other ways of viewing prayer and to explore the significance and potential of this great power in relation to our creative aspirations. And I pray that all I seek to convey may flow to you through the Spirit of the Lord so that you may know with inward assurance that which is true for you.

POWER THOUGHTS

1 Healings and transformations take place through love, faith and prayer. The medical profession is increasingly recognising the validity and importance of spiritual principles in relation to health and healing.

2 Healings also follow the ministrations of doctors, psychiatrists and all who serve the sick through scientific knowledge and techniques.

3 There is a common denominator between spiritual and medical healing which is founded on the whole man of spirit, mind and body. Wisdom demands full co-operation between minister, doctor and patient.

4 Examine your life carefully and, if there is any discord of mind or sickness of body, boldly go forward in love, faith and prayer; and at the same time release these principles in your relationship with the doctors who are also God's instruments of healing.

5 Recall the importance of love and imagination. Set your house in order and hold a vivid "picture" of WHOLENESS in your mind. This is your plan for the Law of Cause and Effect, operating through love, faith and prayer, is in constant operation night and day. Live it! Feel it! Believe in it! And know that the Perfection of God is freely flooding your being.

A DOCTOR'S PRAYER

Jesus . . . said unto them, They that be whole need not a
physician, but they that are sick.—MATTHEW 9: 12.

I turn to Thee for healing of the soul
Ere through an anguished world I take my way.
How can I hope to cure, who am not whole?
How bid the stricken rise, if sick as they?
Hallow my calling, manifest through me
The miracles once wrought in Galilee.

Be Thou my guide along the aisles of pain,
Thy touch be mine upon the fevered brow.
Grant me Thy Wisdom, make Thy Purpose plain
I consecrate my labours to Thee now.
Mine is the human hand, but Thine the skill,
I do but work according to Thy Will.

Make me Thy chalice-bearer, Lord of All,
Brimming with sacred, life-restoring wine.
Lest in some pit of boastful pride I fall
Grant I remember that the Power is Thine.
Oh, weave Thy Pattern through a mortal man,
Using my gifts in Thy immortal plan.

I seek no fading laurel wreaths of fame,
Content to be Thy tempered instrument,
Chosen by Thee to glorify Thy Name,
Treading the healing road Thy mercy went.

*   *   *

Help me to follow in humility
Behind the Healing Christ of Galilee.

"MAC"

Chapter 10

THE CREATIVE POWER OF PRAYER

WITH GREAT INSIGHT, someone has said:
"The teacher, if he is wise, does not bid you to enter the house of his wisdom, but rather leads you to the threshold of your own mind—for the vision of one lends not its wings to another, and even as each one stands alone in God's knowledge, so must each one be alone in his knowledge of God and in his understanding."

We can share our knowledge, vision and experiences and help one another in countless ways, but always our own evolution can proceed only through our own love, faith, choice, and mental processes. That is why in our discussions I have sought only to share, as simply as possible, knowledge about the mind and its functions, and to indicate perhaps simpler ways whereby you can augment your well-being and creative expression. Throughout the main purpose has been to inspire *you* to embark boldly upon the development and use of the exciting gifts inherent in your own being.

It was inevitable that our journey through the known qualities of personality and consciousness should lead us into an appreciation of our spiritual faculties and into the realm of prayer. They are valid human gifts and spiritual experiences, and to ignore them would be like diminishing the illumination of an electric light by darkening half the bulb.

The life power of the individual is like the electric current flowing from the power station which reaches the bulb and irradiates the clear glass to illumine the environment. But, in our personalities, we control the degree and direction of our expression and often fail to use the full potential of the "light" available to us.

Or, to use another example, it is as though the mind is like a shadowed room with one small candle flickering in the corner. The windows are shrouded by heavy curtains which keep out the sunlight beating upon them. Some of us are content to live in our own candlelight and perhaps are not aware of the bright sunshine outside. Others may know of it but choose to ignore its value. But, of course, there are many people who seek in countless ways to allow the greater light to enter their rooms.

The sunshine is beating on the windows for all of us. Prayer is like drawing the curtains and, instantly, the light floods into our room. The illumination we receive depends entirely on the degree to which the curtain is opened. Some, hesitatingly and tentatively, may open only one small space; even so, a flash of light comes in. Others expose a greater gap, and even more sunshine streams through. The wise man, unhesitatingly and boldly, flings back the curtains and his room is radiant with light.

The very fact that man can conceive the possibility of prayer, or communion with God, suggests that he can achieve it, conditioned only by the degree of his vision, his faith and his constant perseverance.

We have established a firm foundation for our faith which springs to life when we pause long enough to be detached from the whirl of self and to behold the intensity of God's presence and action within ourselves and in all creation. Then commonsense comes into focus, and we know the truth without further need of argument or definition.

Having accepted this, the interminable problem has always been *how to pray*, or commune with God, in an effective way. We all believe in an Almighty Creator, but are often very uncertain about our ability to experience His power in our lives.

May I again remind you of a great truth? I believe, confronted by such an immense project as communicating with the Lord, that we tend to make it complicated and thus often defeat our purpose. We become involved so easily in the manifold definitions, methods and means established by so many seekers that we lose sight of the simple truth that *the Father, in His own Being and Purpose, is forever seeking to manifest His Powers in and through us.*

He is limited only by the degree of our human limitations, lack of faith, recognition, and willingness to accept His gifts. In our free-will it is our birthright to decide even the degree to which we embrace and obey Divine laws, and to what extent we believe in the effectiveness of Divine power in our lives.

Since love is fundamental to communion with Love, or God, this must be our first concern. If, as already discussed, we can embrace and obey this Law, then we are in fact ready for effective prayer. It involves repentance, or turning away from all the old mistakes to accept unconditionally the transforming forgiveness of God, the healing of the past, and a new beginning.

True communion always involves us in loving forgiveness of others who may have trespassed against us. And by this I mean a forgiveness based upon a longing for the total well-being of the one who, perhaps in ignorance of Divine laws or through deep compulsions, has hurt us.

"Forgiveness is the perfume the dying flower casts back upon the foot that crushed it."

May I also remove one other obstacle which seems to prevent so many people from a simple and complete experience of answered prayer? Strangely enough, this problem is based on a fallacy, or a wrong concept, and is often most intense among those who are sincerely seeking the highest way to the Lord.

We begin to yearn for the spiritual way and become conscious of the immensity of the project on the one hand, and of our own inadequacy on the other. With a new spiritual understanding we are much more aware of our sins and weaknesses, and feel we have a lot to learn, such a long way to go, before we can even become worthy enough, or able enough, to enter into full communion with the perfect nature of God.

The common cry among Christians is, "Oh! if only I had more faith." "If only I could curb my irritation or be loving enough, good enough, or knew the right way!"

This, of course, is born out of a natural recognition that our true objective is to become spiritually perfect. But we forget one vital truth. We do not have to wait until we are perfect before we can commune with God. If it were so, then we should all have to delay this throughout eternity—for perfection is a quality that unfolds towards unknowable ultimates.

Oh, no! We come to the Lord just as we are, in all our immaturity, with our sins, weaknesses, lack of faith, love, intellect and all else. We come to Him as simply and spontaneously as a child to its father. Hence the need for a great and abiding simplicity, based on a recognition that we live, and move, and have our being in the Spirit of God—now and forever. He knows our every thought, hears our every call, has an infinite plan and purpose for us, and awaits our humble acceptance so that He can release the imprisoned splendour of His Own Perfection into our lives.

Our progression in prayer is best centred in this simple belief. We cannot completely know God, but we can experience His Love and Infinite Nature in every aspect of our personality and way of life. We have enough faith this very hour, provided we can embrace this fundamental truth.

How to Pray Effectively

You and I are now in communion with each other. My mind speaks to yours, and you are experiencing the flow of ideas. I have prayed that the concepts which are true to your nature shall be quickened to your awareness, and I believe sincerely that this has already been realised by you.

Think back for a moment, and trace your thoughts and reactions as you considered all these ideas. Some statements will have stirred you in wonderful ways; others, perhaps, in a lesser degree. With every positive acceptance you will have felt a sweeping sense of well-being, a glow of promise, an assurance of great things in the making.

This is a simple example of love, faith and prayer in action, flowing through the essential stream of consciousness from the Father, through me, and thence to you.

In communion with God we can ask help for ourselves, or for other people. And in both approaches there is always an instantaneous response which flows to meet our need, *according to the wisdom and will of God for our highest and eternal good as He knows it.* The degree of our acceptance depends mainly on our own simplicity of trust and faith.

We should consider for a few moments this "Will of

God", for here, too, we seem so often to limit His response by our uncertainty. Hence again the need for simplicity in the belief that not only does He know best what our eternal good may be, but that He also instantly responds to advance it when we pray.

We are often so immersed in personal problems—and perhaps physical sickness—that we fail to realise the potential magnitude of Divine help or to recognise that, as spiritual beings, we are being led through these troubles as we steadfastly keep our attention stayed upon His Perfection. Or that, as spiritual beings, the movement of God in response to our needs must *first* ensure the well-being of the mind to harmonise our affairs and physical needs.

It should be a completely accepted truth that there is no such thing as unanswered prayer. The moment we turn to the Lord, He responds.

With Jesus Christ we can follow all the teaching about prayer, and you would be wise to read the Gospels again with quickened attention. The significance of "What things soever ye desire, when ye pray, believe that ye receive them" is infinite in potential expression. "If ye shall ask anything in my name, I will do it." "All that I have is thine." "It is your Father's good pleasure to give you the kingdom!"

Here is a way whereby you can attain this high estate, which is your heritage, and prove the truth of what I have been saying. Ask yourself the question: What would I like to ask the Lord to do in partnership with me? Then make a list of all your personal needs, based on what you think is necessary to make your life perfect. Include everything. Your own commonsense and instinct will reveal the basic requirements of health, happiness, and the spiritual and material objectives we have discussed together.

Then, in a quiet time, just accept without question that you are in His Presence. Say, "Here, Lord, are my needs to the best of my ability to realise them. I now give them to You . . . (speak them aloud) . . . Thank You, Father. . . . I understand and accept that You have heard my requests and I am content to leave them in Your care. Please now bring the right answers in the right way, according to Your Will for my highest good, through Jesus Christ."

Place your list in a drawer and leave everything safely in His keeping. From that moment, open your mind with LOVE to the Lord. Worship Him with praise and thanksgiving. And, if worry, pain or other troubles temporarily remain with you, remember that *He* is in charge and that day by day wonderful consequences will promote your well-being.

In a month from now, take out your list and analyse the changes that have taken place. Delete those problems which have been settled, and notice those in which progress has been made. Some may yet remain. Re-draft your list to include any new problems and objectives, give thanks, and put it away for another month, knowing that night and day the infinite love of God is freely and comprehensively working on your behalf. "Thank You, Father, for every perfect answer irresistibly flowing into my experience."

Month by month continue this process of steadfast thanksgiving and recognition of Divine action. So many of our real problems involve other people, changes in our own thoughts and actions, and a sequence of events which are quickened for our good. *Some of our greatest needs are met*

E

*over an extended period because they involve so many factors which
the Father has to adjust to bring forth the perfect answer for all
concerned.* Hence the need for patience, understanding and
a constant practice of the never-failing Presence in relation
to every aspect of our lives and our projects.

Your natural communion with the Lord is a continuing
awareness of His Presence as the centre of all experience.
At any moment you can speak to Him from your heart.
Your awareness becomes so quickened that your life is
rendered to Him in every service, and by watching
carefully for every situation or person for which or for
whom you can ask His help.

As you work in your office or job—or simply cleaning,
cooking, or washing up the dishes—you are in prayer
when you render your service to Him on behalf of others.
Many an inspired thought will then illumine your mind.
Some of the greatest ideas have flashed into people's
minds during the performance of mundane, everyday
tasks.

Walking down a street, or riding in tram or bus you
always have opportunities to pray. A cripple passes by:
"Thank You, Father, for Thy Blessing upon him." And
you can be sure that something wonderful is released to
him. God works through a smile, a kind action, the
extended hand of help or friendship. The essential purpose
of God is to radiate Perfection in illumined thoughts and
actions.

Did you know that you can even pray for the flowers
and plants in your garden? People who love them and
talk to them always produce beautiful blooms. We say
that someone has "green fingers," but the effectiveness of
their creativeness is due to love. If you are a gardener,
behold God in the midst; pray for and love each plant,

and you will see the amazing results. You can even conduct experimental research in this if you like. Those who have done so under controlled conditions all report increased growth and perfection in the vegetables or flowers for which they consistently prayed. All because there is Love.

You can pray when driving your car. I wonder how many accidents would be avoided if we were all upheld in peace and protection, driving always conscious of God's Presence on our journeys? What do *you* think?

We all have our own personal objectives and, of course, a deep instinct to rectify faults and achieve our ends. But, beyond the self, are our relationships with others and their needs. It is in this field that we can truly find our highest expression. Here we have the illimitable opportunity for loving, in all its forms of kindness, tolerance, understanding and service. And, when love is freely flowing, you can be sure that the movement of God is already involved —for God *is* that love.

That is why, when concerned for the well-being of others, our prayer-power functions at its highest level. It leads us into prayer for everyone with whom we live and work, for the people we meet each day and, in the wider sense, for the whole world.

There is no area of human experience or any situation, close at hand or a thousand miles away, which cannot be influenced for good by prayer. Time and distance are no obstacle to effective prayer because all things, and all people, are contained within the One Mind of an Omnipresent Father.

Perhaps the most remarkable discovery of modern times has been the effectiveness of prayer for people and conditions at a distance. This is known as intercession. So important is this that in a later chapter I will quote the individual experiences of just a few of a host of people who, in my own experience, received healing and help because we prayed for them. My knowledge of effective intercession has been extended by similar results noted by others who serve in this way.

You, too, therefore can embark on any prayer project of your choice. You have the same natural ability to pray and to receive God's response as has anyone else. Your only need is to believe it, and to be simple in your recognition and acceptance of the Father's answers.

It is not your responsibility to assess *how* the Lord deals with the needs of others. Too often we pray for someone who may be sick or in trouble and, to outward appearance, the trouble persists; so we think our prayer has not been answered, condemn our own ineffectiveness, and lose faith.

We perhaps did not appreciate that there are often · many aspects of mind and body which may require adjustment within the scope of the free-will personality of the other person. Prayer releases help towards the ultimate solution. Following prayer, many a changed life unfolds over a period of months or even years.

I remember, for instance, praying for a lady at a service in Morecambe. She was crippled with arthritis of many years standing. Outwardly she was just as crippled and in the same pain when she went home as she was when we prayed for her.

Five weeks later the arthritic lady came to my Sanctuary. And there she was—walking, jumping, bending and with great joy demonstrating to me how completely she had been healed. She told me that during the intervening five weeks her entire life had been centred on loving people, worshipping God's Presence, believing in His Perfection and rendering to Him every possible service in the home and to her family. Day by day her body became increasingly released until complete freedom came. She came to give thanks for the prayer and teaching which had made it possible.

At services or in private counselling I always seek to evoke an understanding of the spiritual principles we have been discussing here. Then we pray, knowing that at least some of the truth and responsibility involved in our communion with the Lord has been accepted.

When you pray for anyone—just pray with love and trust, and thereafter leave everything to Him, constantly giving thanks that Perfect Everything is flowing in the way HE decrees.

This is now a good moment for you to make a list of the people for whom you would like to seek God's Blessing. You might also like to include everyone on earth, and specific local or world problems. Then, with all love and simplicity, hold your list in your hands, and pray—"Thank You, Father. In my love for Thee and for all these people, I release their needs into Thy keeping. Thank You, Lord, that Thy Perfection will be shining, night and day, in each of them, to bring forth their highest good in ways which flow in accordance with Thy will and knowledge of each one."

Put your list away and daily thank God for the Blessings that flow to them. And, as you meet or contact those for whom you pray, watch carefully for the changes that will take place.

In some, perhaps, the pain will have gone. Others will demonstrate a greater peace, love, friendship or courage. Sure enough, you will see signs to tell you that your prayer is receiving an active response if you look for this with spiritual sensitivity and perception.

Your experiences in this infinite undertaking will be as constant as your dedication and application. The water in a faucet is always there, and the pipes go right back to a reservoir which stores millions of gallons for your use. But the water will flow only when the tap is turned on!

Before we go on to discuss God's Healing and Creative Silence, I should like you to ponder the Power Thoughts that now follow.

Thank you, Father.

POWER THOUGHTS

1 Effective prayer is based on love for God and for people. It is centred in a faith so simple that we can accept the Presence as effortlessly as the air we breathe, the world around us, the sunshine, or our own beings. We live in the Presence of God. The Kingdom is within you.

2 Prayer is communion with God, believing in instant contact and acceptance of a response which is Perfect Everything for our highest and eternal Good, according to His knowledge of our true needs.

3 "What things soever ye desire, when ye pray, *believe that ye receive them* and ye shall have them." Since Jesus said this, accept it as a fact.

4 Examine today what you believe to be your real needs. Talk, spontaneously, to God as a living Presence. Then just thank Him for a constant response which is healing, guiding and helping in every situation. Observe the results of your prayer as events unfold. Go confidently into this day, this week, knowing that the Lord goes with you.

5 Take your long-term objectives. Begin with your
personality, go right through all your relationships,
and decide what you believe to be your true aims.
Ask the Father to take charge and unfold them in
you and through you step by step. Give constant
thanksgiving that you are being swept forward to
perfect accomplishment.

THE GREATER WORKS

He that believeth on me, the works that I do shall he do also;
and greater works than these shall he do; because I go unto
my Father.—JOHN 14: 12.

> I Blessed a cup of water in His Name
> And 'twas transmuted to a draught Divine.
> I never saw Him enter . . . yet He came
>   To turn it into wine.
>
> I gave a morsel from my scanty store,
> Nor knew I was bestowing Heav'nly food.
> Lo! at His touch it multiplied the more
>   And fed a multitude.
>
> I lit a candle in the troubled night
> Of earth's vast darkness; as it glimmered there
> Before me stretched a radiant road of light. . . .
>   The Lord had heard my prayer.
>   "MAC"

Chapter 11

THE CREATIVE POWER OF SILENCE

I BECOME QUIET and, without effort, relax in the Presence of God. A deep silence enfolds me. It is so intense I can almost "listen" to it!

Because your mind is tuned to mine at this moment through the printed word, it is inevitable that through the One Mind of God in which we both exist you also will be enveloped in the same Peace.

For a few moments relax and, quite simply, accept that you are poised and centred in the Spirit of God—and "listen" to the stillness which instantly steals over you—Peace—Quietness—Listen!

* * *

Much has been written about meditation because the principle of abiding in God's Presence has been known and practised down the ages. All who have cultivated this way of communion with God report healing, inspiration and power flowing into their lives.

Meditation is a realistic experience with practical and positive influences on the personality and mind. It always promotes our well-being and opens ways to creative fulfilment far beyond the capacity of our own powers.

Innumerable methods and means have been advocated by many ministers, mystics and others who have discovered this truth through dedication and practice. They all point to the Blessings which are released when, with worship, love and praise, we turn our attention to the Presence of God and abide, or become still, in Him.

Throughout our fellowship I have deliberately sought to eliminate all complications and controversy in relation to the psychological functions of the mind and its basic spiritual outreach. I have endeavoured to point out simple truths common to all and equally available to all. Every student, minister or member of any denomination can directly apply them as central to, and within the pattern of, every religious practice.

Now as we turn our attention to the vital subject of meditation, I would ask that we approach it in simplicity, the key to so many religious practices. While saying this I have no wish to deny the validity of other existing methods of meditation.

I accept and believe that the all-pervading Spirit, Intelligence and Will of God, dwelling within us and all round us, is forever yearning to infuse our lives with all the love, wisdom, intellectual power, inspiration, knowledge and help we need at any time to secure our well-being, and to help us to fulfil the purposes that are our true objectives here on earth, and beyond.

The sunshine which bathes the earth with light belongs to us all. We experience it as "daylight." We can come effortlessly out of our dark rooms and when we feel the sun's warm rays our awareness is intensified. The light and warmth reach us automatically; we merely offer ourselves to them.

In meditation we need to realise the same simple truth because, in our uncertainty, we tend to seek complicated ways whereby we can, as it were, become good enough, or proficient enough to "break-through" to God.

Our ideas are radically changed when we can understand and accept that it is *God Who seeks to fill our lives with His Perfect Nature*, and that our part is merely to present ourselves to His Presence, to recognise and accept the good *He* initiates and releases to us in His Love.

The more educated we become the more do we incline to evolve complicated ideas. This is specially true when man conceives the possibility of communicating with the Creator of the Universe. It is seemingly so vast a project that man becomes involved in profound theological thinking and often originates exclusive methods whereby we can best reach Him.

In the various suggested methods we tend to lose sight of the simple truth, placing little reliance upon simplicity itself. This is a great mistake for it makes our way forward very difficult. When we proclaim a loving Father of all mankind, surely He is equally available to everyone. If our Christianity has become too complicated for many of us then, indeed, has our approach been unnecessarily involved.

We should be able to come to the Father as a child to its parent without waiting until we are grown-up and become "clever." And, likewise, we should know the constant supervising care of the Lord just as earthly parents watch over *their* children.

In meditation I believe the only real problem is how to help each other to accept the rule of simplicity. Words are so inadequate to convey the heights and depths of abiding in God. And, moreover, we are often so caught up in the complications of living that there seems to be no direct way to the answer—so we continue to dwell in the complexities and uncertainties of consciousness.

When we become still, just abiding in the Presence, a

fundamental expression of God takes place. A deep stillness, peace, and quietness enfold us. You must have experienced this yourself many times. Have you never gone into a church, out of the busy street, and instantly felt the deep contrasting peace? This "atmosphere" of a church is real, even though intangible. I often slip into an empty church while travelling and become instantly lifted up in the prevailing Peace. Many of my problems have thus subsequently been solved. The enfolding peace is often specially intense just before a service begins, when the congregation is quietly sitting in prayer.

What I seek to convey to you is this: that whenever we present ourselves to the Lord, the immediate response is Peace—Stillness. So many of us miss the significance of this, and few expect anything wonderful to happen just because they have experienced something as simple as stillness. We fail to recognise that this is the Peace, Harmony and Perfection of God actually offering to us the fullness of His Perfect Nature.

The only reality we ever know is that which we can conceive, believe and accept. If, therefore, we only accept the quietness as a more or less natural state, enjoying it as a rest from activity, then that becomes the level of its reality to us. If, on the other hand, we recognise and accept that the Perfection of God is flowing through mind, body and environment, demonstrated in this stillness, then this becomes reality.

Let me digress for a few moments to view this from another direction. Comfortable? Remember we are relaxing together in the Presence of God. Even as we share these thoughts great Blessings are flowing to us both. Sit back in your chair—let go—and you will feel more content, peaceful and happy than perhaps for a long time. With every communion like this there is always a deep sense of well-being and hope for the future. Feel it?

Now think back over the years. You will have passed through periods of stress, worry, pain, sickness, unhappiness and perhaps even despair. So you know the disturbing tensions of all these troubles. When they come you are disturbed in mind, and often in a state of acute strain. A sick body is disordered or in dis-ease. Your mind is chaotic, fraught with worry, fear, distress or conflict.

What is the exact opposite of all tension, stress, dis-ease, conflict? Surely it is Peace, Harmony, Order, Wholeness?

Jesus said, "My Peace I give unto you, not as the world giveth"—but MY Peace, the Perfect Nature of My Own Being.

In John 15: 7, He says, "If ye abide in me (become still and constantly present yourself to my Presence) and my words abide in you (your acceptance and obedience to His instructions about love, faith and prayer), ye shall ask what ye will, and it shall be done unto you."

Here, then, is the significance of the Silence. As we abide in His Presence the Divine Peace flows in, and through, and all about us. The purpose is to bring Divine Order into our lives, to resolve conflict in reconciliation, chaos in peace, sickness in health, failure in success, worry in trust and every disturbance in all-embracing PEACE.

We are involved in a developing life, meeting every kind of experience. Our general attitudes and reactions are fundamental to every event, for good or ill, as we choose. If we expose ourselves to negative influences we become disturbed accordingly. If we are exposed to the constant flow of Divine Love, Peace, Harmony and positive influences, so are we helped in this direction.

That is why true meditation should be a constant awareness of God's Presence. It is not enough, for example, to experience His Peace in church on Sunday morning, and then allow ourselves to be entangled in any snare which comes during the week.

Every day we should seek to spend a few minutes in the stillness, and so develop a deeper awareness of the constant Presence in all we are doing. Then His Peace will be present in all our activities, and His love, inspiration, guidance and infinite good will be manifest always.

You may well ask, "But how can I do this when I am so busy all day?" Granted, but if you have accepted what I have said to be true then you will discover that His presence is similar to an awareness of daylight. For instance, *I am concentrating on expressing my thoughts in words*, but I am also aware of deep peace and God's Presence, and all those things that make up my environment.

You may now also question, "Yes, I understand all this, and accept the fact of God's Presence. But how do I do it? Whenever I have tried before, my mind wanders, I fidget, and somehow never seem to get the contact you speak about. What is wrong?"

Perhaps again I should guide you back to simplicity. So many people worry about the flow of thoughts which detract from a contemplation of God, and believe they thus fail in meditation. I think these people are mistaken.

If you sit in a deck chair in the sunshine, you are immediately sunbathing. The important thing was the placing of yourself in the warm rays. Thereafter the light shines on you, irrespective of whether you go to sleep, plan a picnic next week, or remember a recent party. The sun shines, *of its own volition*, all the time you remain there.

So now, why not be still, relaxed and comfortable. "Lord, I am in Thy Presence now, with all love, just to abide in Thee, open to Thy Perfection. Thank You, Father, for now my mind, body and affairs are under Thy dominion and perfect everything flows according to Thy Will, to meet every need."

This means that you are now abiding in God. Whatever your mundane thoughts, your purpose was accomplished by your decision. The Lord knows all about you. He ministers to you irrespective of your thinking processes, movements or sleep. And Peace will cover every aspect of your life.

We are so sure in our recognition that we are now giving God all our trust and love. We are reaching the highest level of faith because we accept completely that He desires, in His Love for us, to minister unto our every need. He does so according to the degree we accept His Perfection.

This is so important that I should like to share another picture which may help you. Suppose, instead of something as simple as a stillness, a blazing gold-white Light shone all round us when we meditated or prayed. It would be so startling in its revelation of Divine Splendour that we would have no difficulty in establishing an all-embracing faith in His Presence. And we would all be instantly healed of every kind of ill that afflicted us. When you pray, or meditate, let your imagination behold this Glory. Think of your chair blazing in that Light. Sit, relax, and believe that you are centred in, and receiving, the Perfection of Christ as you abide in His Spirit.

Like everything to which we devote our close attention the knowledge of it deepens as we consistently bear it in mind. This is particularly true of meditation, being still in God, because our minds are *changed for us*. We become quickened with Divine Thoughts, and inspiration, guidance and creative powers come to us in relation to our way of life. It is everyman's potential highway to healing, and creative positive thinking—Power Thinking with God.

The more we accept the positive Powers of God being directed into our lives the more easily shall we be able to cease our striving to "think" our way to Him.

There are, as we have discussed, many methods of prayer. We can talk to the Lord, person to person, and tell Him of our troubles, hopes and needs. We can worship Him with praise and adoration. We can find Him in our work and our relationships, even among the pots and pans, and in all other everyday activities. But when we seek to become still, there are three simple ways to come to Him:

(1) Just accept God, asking nothing, but leaving everything to Him as we abide in His Presence. We are not concerned about self or what we are thinking, asleep or awake. Only abiding, as effortlessly as a baby in its mother's arms.

(2) We relax in the Presence. The Peace comes. We have some questions about a problem, situation, or trouble. We ask the Lord, as a Presence, for the answer. Then we listen, and let go our thoughts. Having asked, willing to accept His solution, we know the answer will be forthcoming. Perhaps in the Silence as you relax; perhaps

through events, a book, or other people. But the answer will come. "Ask, and it shall be given you; seek, and ye shall find; knock, and it shall be opened unto you" (Luke 11: 9). All knowledge, about anything and everything, is centred in God.

(3) In the Silence of the Spirit—be still—and LISTEN. Just listen to God, listen to the stillness—and the still, small Voice, coming in silent thoughts, will bring you inspiration from Him. Perhaps you will remember someone not seen for a long time. God's Blessing flows to that person. Thank You, Father. . . . The germ of an idea about your business, research work, or other project, begins to formulate. Listen! The Father knows exactly how to communicate with you in many ways.

"And I heard a great voice out of heaven saying, Behold, the tabernacle of God is with men, and he will dwell with them, and they shall be his people, and God himself shall be with them, and be their God.

"And God shall wipe away all tears from their eyes; and there shall be no more death, neither sorrow, nor crying, neither shall there be any more pain; for the former things are passed away.

"And he that sat upon the throne said, Behold, I make all things new. And he said unto me, Write: for these words are true and faithful."—Rev. 21: 3, 5. A.V.

*   *   *

To give you some illustrations of the truth of what I have been saying of God's willingness to answer prayer, I intend to quote some stories which witness His Power. But first let us dwell on some of the points we have discussed in this chapter.

POWER THOUGHTS

1 We live, and move, and have our being in the Spirit of God. There is no place where He is not. He is the Creator of all, and therefore it is His Purpose to unfold the plan and purpose of your life.

2 Being still in the Presence is to accept that God yearns to unfold our highest good and open our hearts to His Perfection so that He can be expressed in our lives.

3 Spend a few minutes, morning and night, just resting in God, knowing that His Peace represents Divine order, love, wholeness, joy, strength, courage, success, harmony, faith and power.

4 Observe the changes in your daily life. And, later, recognise the new ideas and the balanced personality which you are becoming.

5 This can be accomplished only through practice. But rest assured it is the way forward and vital to your true well-being and final objectives.

THE HEALING SILENCE

Be still, and know that I am God.—PSALM 46: 10.

Thank God for silence, when all words are spoken,
The thoughtless, foolish, wounding words we say.
Now, may the healing quiet be unbroken,
We would be still, and let Him have His way.

Thank God for silence, when all tears are ended,
The tears we cause by acts beyond recall.
Now, in this healing hour the hurts are mended.
Behold, He comes! And we forget them all.

Thank God for silence when, our faults confessing,
Lowly we kneel and strife and turmoil cease.
On downbent heads we feel His Healing Blessing—
And turn, and take the pathway of His Peace.

                                    "MAC"

Chapter 12

HEALING AND ANSWERED PRAYER

I SAT ON the rostrum of the vast Methodist Central Hall in Westminster, London, and contemplated the three thousand people assembled there in an electric atmosphere of anticipation.

The mass of people on the floor of the hall was balanced by those on the crowded balconies rising all round to the roof. The high platform seemed almost to be suspended in the midst of a multitude of minds focussing their combined attention on this central point.

It was an exquisite and revealing experience to be identified with such a gathering of personalities whose interest was intent upon exploring and assessing spiritual truths. It was fascinating to observe the scene of faces, the splashes of colour of the ladies' dresses and hats contrasting with the more sombre clothing of the men, often enhanced by flashes of sunshine through the high windows.

But far beyond this was the tremendous impact and awareness of the power of the minds of all these people, blending in eager concentration on the speakers. I knew, with a deep and innate insight that, in the end, it would always be the family men and women of the world who would accept, decree and motivate every advance in spiritual progress.

We had assembled in the Central Hall for a "Healing

Teach-In" organised by the National Federation of Spiritual Healers. Its purpose was to provide an opportunity for a free exchange of ideas by leaders of the various Ministries of Healing, and to show that all methods and approaches—spiritual or medical—*are complementary and not competitive.*

To this end twenty-two speakers had been invited to express their views. They represented the following denominations.

Anglican Church.
    Canon J. D. Pearce-Higgins, M.A.
    (Vice-Provost of Southwark Cathedral).
    The Rev. R. A. Bontoft De St. Quentin, M.A.
    (Vicar of Cholsey, Berkshire).

The Methodist Church.
    The Rev. The Lord Soper, M.A., Ph.D.
    (Superintendent Minister of the West London Mission).
    The Rev. Dr. Maurice Barnett, M.A., B.D.
    (Principal Minister of the Methodist Central Hall, London).
    The Rev. Dr. Leslie Weatherhead, C.B.E., M.A., Ph.D., D.Litt., D.D.
    (Minister-Emeritus, The City Temple, London).

The Churches' Fellowship for Psychical and Spiritual Studies.
    The Rev. Bertram E. Woods
    (Hon. General Secretary).
    Lt. Col. R. M. Lester, F.J.I.
    (Founder and Chairman).

The Catholic Church.
    Father D. E. Konstant, M.A.
    (Westminster Catholic Diocesan Inspector of Schools).

Society of Friends (Quaker).
    Mrs. Phyllis Taunton Wood
    (Chairman of the Friends' Healing Guild).

Spiritualist Churches and Healers.

Mr. Harry Edwards
(President of the National Federation of Spiritual Healers).
Mr. Gordon Turner
(Chairman of the National Federation of Spiritual Healers).
Mr. Maurice Barbanell
(Editor of "Psychic News" and "Two Worlds").
Mrs. Ella Sheridan
(President of the Greater World Spiritual Healers' Guild).
Mr. Eric Stuart
(President of the Spiritualist Association of Great Britain).
Dr. John Winning
(President of the Spiritualist National Union Healers' Guild).

Buddhism.

Mr. Maurice Walshe, M.A.
(Chairman of the Buddhist Sangha Association).

Interested Public Personalities.

Dr. Brian St. John Inglis
(Editor "Spectator" 1959–62, and television personality).
Mr. Beverley Nichols
(Author).
Mr. George Rogers, C.B.E., M.P.

Doctors—Unofficially representing the medical profession.
One doctor incognito.
Mr. Arthur Dickson Wright, M.S., F.R.C.S.
(Past Vice-President of the Royal College of Surgeons).

Inter-Denominational.

Brother Mandus
(Leader—World Healing Crusade).

I participated in the entire proceedings from 10.30 a.m. until 8.45 p.m., and listened with intense interest to all the speakers and their freely expressed ideas about spiritual and medical healing.

My aim here is not to report the specific words of each speaker but rather humbly to draw what I believe to be some significant conclusions.

Several central factors were emphasised in clear perspective:—

(1) A general agreement about the validity of healings, following all the various spiritual approaches i.e. the orthodox church, prayer, faith, psychic and mental.

(2) Considerable disagreement between the orthodox church and the spiritualist views about methods.

(3) All spiritual leaders expressed the desire for recognition and closer collaboration with the medical profession.

(4) The doctors present, although not officially representing their profession, agreed with the validity of spiritual healing and its objectives.

All day I was conscious of the three thousand absorbed people all round us listening to these views with intense attention. And again I knew, beyond all the claims of church, denomination, or doctors, that it would be they alone who would eventually decide which way could best help them to be healed or to benefit their spiritual lives.

The speakers were radiant with sincerity and conviction about the wondrous reality of their individual experiences in this field of discovery. For they knew that their approach was founded on the fact that people had been healed, often of so-called incurable diseases, by their ministrations.

I felt an overwhelming compassion for those who suffer, and a tremendous longing for agreement between all conflicting human opinions on how God works to help those in need.

The entire Christian Church is founded on love, compassion, tolerance and the healing of broken minds and bodies. And here, in our own day and age, we again have the undeniable evidence of countless healings taking place through every spiritual approach—whether by orthodox or unorthodox channels.

Here, at least, is basic evidence of powers beyond human understanding, flowing to heal the sick whenever love, faith or prayer are released in a yearning to help them. The records prove that this is not conditioned by the methods employed or the kind of church which formulates them.

It is vital to realise that no single denomination, church, group or individual has a monopoly of spiritual healing and we must honestly assess why this is so, and lift our vision to embrace its significance. Common-sense, and the urgency of the deep needs of this age, urge upon us a much more realistic appreciation of the basic truth and potentials inherent in all aspects of spiritual and medical healing.

The real error which has pursued and dominated the fragmented Christian and spiritual scene is based on a misunderstanding of human nature itself. As outlined earlier in this book, everyone is an individual in his own right and must, therefore, express himself according to the pattern of his experience and interest. This inevitably means that we are involved in as many variations of personality as there are people. And, moreover, we are all on various levels of evolving understanding throughout the whole vast field of human expression.

For this reason alone we have a thousand differing denominations in the Christian scene, to say nothing of other religions; and the leaders and their congregations are deeply rooted in allegiance, belief and sincerity.

So profound is this truth that it will never be possible to pour human personality into ONE spiritual mould.

People, inevitably, will always follow their interest, inclination and the patterns which seem best suited to their needs.

Surely our true way forward is to accept and understand this, and to establish an absolute respect for the works of all people who are seeking to serve and help humanity in every spiritual way? We are then not involved in judgment, but rather in developing our own church pattern to the maximum of its love-potential. We may thus be one with all others in spirit, in tolerance and respect without ever wishing to emulate them in their chosen way—or they in ours.

I was led, on this platform, to express this underlying unity, and to call forth the central responsibility of love, tolerance, faith and prayer.

In fact, in deep meditation, you can assess it for yourself. I told the assembly, "If your brother, desperately diseased, was healed through the ministration of a psychic healer, would you cry because he had not been succoured through your own different belief and approach? If your sister was healed by a surgeon operating on her body, would you be unhappy because his way was different from your spiritual belief in Divine Healing?"

In the end people will lead their leaders into ways that are realistic and produce the highest good. People will always follow the way which appeals to their love, faith and imagination—*and each way will be right for them at the time of their approach, even though they may change to other views later.*

Christianity, in all its forms of expression, will no longer be fragmented by discord and disagreement when we see and accept the truth of spiritual unity based on tolerance, respect and co-operation. Then each church will concentrate on cultivating its own particular spiritual potentials to the maximum, strengthened by undergirding unity with all others, and quickened by every exciting experience or advance which others may make in their progressive unfoldment.

When we add to this the secure knowledge that the new horizons for mankind are inevitably founded on spiritual values, we can leap forward with conviction and authority. When each church knows and implements this vision of the scientific reality of spiritual principles in relation to the well-being and evolution of mankind, then indeed we shall see the real dawn of a new age.

The "Teach-in" closed with a minute of Silent Prayer, and the Great Stillness of God swept over us all as we waited upon Him . . . and in the Silence, His voice was louder than the voices of men. And I knew that these people, and all mankind, one by one, were equally loved and equally important to Him.

* * *

In our inter-denominational work through our World Healing Crusade which has its headquarters at The Sanctuary, 476 Lytham Road, Blackpool, Lancs., England, the evidence mounts daily of the harmonising and beneficial effects of Love and Prayer for the restoration of health. I now intend to quote some true testimonies which are not only similar but endorse the stories I heard at the "Healing Teach-In". I should like to start with a moving account of answered prayer as told by the Rev. John Williams of the Congregational Church, Eastbourne:

"This story concerns our child Paul. He was fourteen months old at the time. It was late on Saturday night or rather early on Sunday morning, when we were disturbed by a noise in his cot and found him in convulsive fits.

"As early as possible in the morning we got the doctor, who diagnosed meningitis. I went to my service as usual. Later in the afternoon a second opinion was sought and it was decided that the meningitis was not cerebral where you could have administered a serum, or mastoid where they might have operated, but tubercular. There was no sort of treatment nor any kind of cure.

"He was whisked off to Great Ormond Street Hospital in London. When I got back to my service at night, all unknown to me, our church secretary had invited the congregation, having told them what had happened, to remain for prayer after the service, and everybody did. The whole congregation was in prayer, many taking part audibly who might never have heard their voices raised in public before.

"I went down to the hospital on Monday and the surgeon confirmed what was the matter and advised me not to come any more, as the boy couldn't live more than two days. 'Well,' I said, 'I would like to see him if I may.' He said, 'You can if you want to. You might come to-morrow, because Tuesdays and Fridays are the days when our brain surgeon is here.'

"When the brain surgeon reported to me on the Tuesday, he confirmed the diagnosis of my own doctor, and the second doctor, and the house surgeon. He said that at the moment my boy was totally quiescent, but not to build any hopes because the tubercular germ did rest and then resumed its damage.

"My boy's eyes were blind. They flashed torches in them and no reaction. They shouted in his ear; he was deaf; they pinched his stomach but there was no reaction.

His brain was absolutely dead. He had got himself twisted into a ball, his head backwards almost touching his feet, which were also bent back.

"I went again on Friday for a second visit to the surgeon, and he said, 'It is remarkable! We have done nothing, and the boy has straightened out.'

"There he was, straightened out, clapping hands, because 'Daddy comes, with a pocket full of plums', a little song which we had taught him.

"On Sunday I announced this miracle to the people. We had a service of thanksgiving. On Tuesday I saw the surgeon again and he said, 'He is well! You might take him home tomorrow'. In my excitement I left his clothes behind in the tube, but eventually got him home. Our own doctor was shocked to think he was back again, and warned me that if he was the least bit sick to send for him at once.

"We forgot that he had been ten days in a ward, and took him out into the sun where he became sick. We 'phoned the doctor and whipped him off to Great Ormond Street in an ambulance where I was reprimanded by the house surgeon, because, he said, they never discharged anyone who was not cured. They said they would keep him until Friday when the brain surgeon was due. We were then told that it was merely a touch of the sun. The boy was perfectly well. On the following day we took him on our summer vacation to Wales. Apart from having a broken nose adjusted at his school, my boy has never seen a doctor since. He is now 27, and is touring India with the grandson of Mahatma Gandhi, helping to morally rearm that great country."

You will be interested to read the following extracts of letters from people for whom we prayed:

"A few months ago the doctors in Ceylon said that my brother would only live for five years because he was suspected of having cancer. It was then that my sister wrote to you, and the day you replied the X-rays showed an improvement. Now he is totally cured."—*S.S., Ceylon*.

"I did tell Brother Mandus when he was down here in April that when I took the chair for him at Westbourne, while he was talking and I was on the platform with him, an electric shock passed right through me. The result, I discovered later, was that my arthritis had been cured."—*Mr. H. M. W., Bournemouth*.

"One very blessed experience we had was when I was talking to a close friend about your work and the efficacy of prayer. She is an English woman also, and has suffered with dermatitis of the hands ever since she was a child of nine years. Lo, and behold! Her skin trouble disappeared immediately while we were talking, and she has never had a return of it. That was well over 18 months ago."—*C. C., Australia*.

"My friend asked me if I knew of your work, and I told her of your ministry at a healing service at Emmanuel Church in Cleveland in the United States. A condition of bleeding that I had had for years was healed, and the operation to stop it was cancelled."—*Mrs. J. McD., Jamaica, W.I.*

"I felt the power of prayer when I went to the Milton Hall, Manchester, with fibrositis in my back. It was very stiff with pain, but when I stood up with others who were sick and we prayed, the very air was still. I felt a wonderful feeling as though a hand was on my back, and then the pain went and it has not come back."—*Mrs. C. W., Levenshulme, Manchester 19.*

"Thank you, dear Brother Mandus, for your prayers, and I thank Almighty God for answering them and for healing me. I wrote to you in August last year to pray for me about my sickness and acute pains in my head and chest, of which sometimes I thought I was going to die. But before I received a reply from you, dear Brother, your prayers had been answered already, and I had been completely healed. This is a miracle, isn't it? I thank God, and I thank the Prayer Group. I hope you will continue to pray for me in what I ask in the name of Jesus. May God bless you. Amen." —*A. E., Ghana.*

"I have received great Blessings on my eyes which I wrote to you about. A few days after I received your letter something suddenly happened to my left eye. It happened one morning when I was meditating, deep in thought. At that moment something fell into my mouth at the back of my throat. I looked at it amazed. It was a piece of skin the shape of my eye, with a small ball of blood at one end. I am sure without doubt that it came from my eye. I thank God for the wonderful way He works through His disciples."—*Mrs. G., Birmingham.*

"Thank you so much for your uplifting and kind letters and prayers. I am happy to report that I went to see my friend and when she showed me her right foot, I saw that the gangrene in her toes, bar the tip of one toe, had completely healed. A new skin has grown over the toes and the affected part of the sole of her foot. A month ago, when the trouble started, the specialist said the toes would have to be removed. He is amazed now and her own doctor said, 'It's a miracle'."—*Mrs. G. A., London.*

"I want to share with you the wonderful answer to prayer which I have had in the past few weeks. I wrote to you for prayer for the skin irritation I had. I went to the doctor and he said it was psoriasis. There was no cure, and I would always have it. Thanks for your prayers because I can tell you the burning and itching has gone and my arm is well. All the redness has gone. Thanks to Our Father."—*Miss H., Tennessee, U.S.A.*

"By the way, I am so glad and I thank the Almighty Lord for He has healed me. Yes, Brother Mandus, when you came to Bandarawela, Ceylon, for your healing session, you laid your hands on me and prayed, and immediately I felt something cooling through the whole of my body. I am cured. Thank God for His wondrous Blessings."—*A.J., Ceylon.*

"And now I have some wonderful news to relate. In my last letter I asked for your prayers, dear Brother, as I was in intense pain from an attack of shingles. The following day at 3 o'clock in the afternoon all pain suddenly left me, and I stood amazed at the wonderful relief. I like to think this happened at the moment you placed my letter on the altar in the Sanctuary, for in the morning your comforting reply came to say you had done so."—*P.A.*

"I am writing this with deep gratitude and thankfulness to God and to you, dear Brother Mandus, for the wonderful miraculous healing that has taken place in my brother. During your Divine Healing Services in Colombo in January this year, my brother was in hospital with a serious lung trouble. The specialist who treated him had taken several X-rays of his lungs, and after many investigations had found out that there was a growth in his lungs which might spread to the bronchial tubes. The surgeon suggested a major operation, but owing to my brother's advanced age it was abandoned and he was asked to take a course of injections. But within a few days the growth disappeared and he was asked to leave the hospital. Although my brother wanted to come to your meetings in Colombo during his stay in hospital, he was unable to do so. But my good friend Miss D. had gone to your meeting and had asked you to pray for him. I am quite confident that it is by your intercession for him that he is cured. Thank You, Father. And thank you, Brother Mandus, for your visit to Ceylon and for your special prayers for our sick people in Ceylon, who may have all been blessed by God through your intercession."—*M.R., Colombo, Ceylon.*

"Thank you for your very welcome letter. You will be happy to know that the little girl I wrote about with osteomyelitis is running about quite trouble free—no leg brace or anything."—*Mrs. E.E., Carnforth.*

"You will be pleased to hear that D.J., the young lad I wrote to you about with possible cancer in the leg, and with the possibility of him losing his leg, has been pronounced perfectly fit. There is no doubt that he was in a very serious condition at the time when I first wrote to you.

I thank you, on behalf of all concerned, for your prayers which have been answered so wonderfully."—*D.C., Ontario, Canada.*

"Last November a friend sent in my name to your Sanctuary when I was suffering from Meniere's disease. The doctor treated me with medicines for over eighteen months and said the dizzy attacks would continue all my life, and get worse. Two days after my name was sent to you the attacks miraculously ceased, and this Spring I have been able to do my own house-decorating and ceiling painting, thanks be to God! My heart is indeed overflowing for all the mercies received and, although on pension, God wonderfully supplies my every need. My prayers morning and evening ascend continually, that God may bless your labours and the work of the World Healing Crusade."—*Miss E.S., Eastham, Cheshire.*

"My friend came to give me the check-up report on her husband, our magistrate, who just about a year ago underwent a very critical heart operation in hospital. At the time I wrote requesting the prayers of your Sanctuary on his behalf, and he made a very wonderful recovery, making medical history. He then went to hospital from 2 p.m. to 6 p.m. and had a really good overhaul, and was told, 'You are a super-phenomenon and you have no business to be alive.' His wife said to me, 'It is just prayer that has saved him'. We thank God. And we thank you, dear Brother Mandus, for your help."—*Miss L.B., Graaff Reinet, South Africa.*

"During the month I was baby sitting. My married daughter was ill in bed. I took her little daughter aside and said, 'We'll pray for Mummie's recovery', and did so as simply as we could, and we both thanked God for an answer to our prayer. In less than three minutes, 'Mummie' appeared fully dressed and proceeded to get dinner, cooking for her family. That is the quickest answer I have had! Bless my little girl partner in prayer and above all—Thank You, Father."—*Mr. E.H., North Vancouver, B.C.*

"I am writing to your Healing Crusade firstly to tell you of the improvement which took place in my son Thomas. When you visited South Africa I attended a service. Thomas has been improving ever since. Thomas was a very slow child, he could only speak at six and found it very difficult to learn at school. He can now read English and Afrikaans, and do easy arithmetic and other school subjects. Thank You, Father, for your Blessings. Thank you for all your prayers and kind sacrifice of time, for all those in need."—*Mrs. A.F., Transvaal, S. Africa.*

"I should like you to know that the gentleman I asked prayers for six months ago, for skin trouble he has had over a period of thirty years, is totally cured, and can hardly believe it. He could not even wear any garment more than one day, because of discharge. Now all his skin is healed and soft. A big—Thank You, Father."—*E.V.R., Prestatyn, Flint.*

Power Thoughts

1 Every physical healing that is brought about by the application of spiritual principles is realised through calling upon Divine help through prayer. When fully understood and accepted, this truth will one day set men free.

F

2 There can be no greater concept for mankind, and his multiplying creativeness, than the knowledge that he can communicate with the infinite Intelligence of the universe and thereby receive a dynamic response.

3 Pause to consider the testimonies in this chapter and appreciate that they are but a fraction of the world's answer to prayer. Be convinced that your prayers will also be answered. Pray every day for your every need, and give thanks for the perfect answer which is flowing to you now.

4 As you grow in faith widen your horizons to embrace the needs of other people and the unity of all churches in Christ. Let tolerance and love be your constant expression but be ever aware of your own Christian responsibilities.

THE FAITH THAT MOVES MOUNTAINS

I have all faith, so that I could remove mountains . . .
—1 CORINTHIANS 13: 2.

I never doubt the easing of my pain
But claiming wholeness, simply trust in Thee;
Nor deem my supplication is in vain
Since Thou hast promised me.

My hunger ne'er shall go unsatisfied,
With Heav'nly manna I am ever fed.
I have Thy word that there will be supplied
My consecrated bread.

Poised in Thy Power, the mightiest task is done,
For 'tis Thy Will, and I can rest content;
Seeing the goal in sight, the victory won,
Perfect accomplishment.

Gladly I journey, though the hour grows late,
Knowing not dread that I may cease to be.
Enfolded in Thy Peace I shall but wait
To greet the dawn with Thee.

"MAC"

Chapter 13

WHAT DO *YOU* THINK?

IN MY FELLOWSHIP with you I have endeavoured to bring to your notice a host of ideas which represent what *I* think. But the more important question is what you have absorbed and—"What do *you* think?"

Through the printed word we have been united in an interchange of spiritual and personal concepts. In this exchange of thoughts I have been endeavouring to show you what has been true in my experience, but it is *you* in whom I am primarily interested. Perhaps you will recall we started the discussion in the comfort of your own home, and so I am now prompted to ask you what you have accepted or rejected. It is more than probable that you have not agreed to all I have proposed, or you may have reservations about some points. This is understandable for when we are dealing with such vast subjects as the mind, health, faith, prayer and Almighty God, you must have many queries you would like to raise. Unfortunately this is not possible for our point of contact is only in conscious thought, yet this can be as real as if we were speaking together by your fireside. An idea accepted could well change the whole of your life as it has done for so many people down the centuries.

In our next, final talk together I want to show you how ideas and ideals, once accepted, can set in motion the machinery for tolerance and understanding among nations of the democratic world. Of course I refer here to the United Nations which, in spite of its shortcomings, has the seed of well-being and peace for all mankind.

The United Nations Organisation is far from perfect and yet it represents the acceptance of the majority of a number of Christian principles which could, if implemented, change the world situation. But before I turn to the "Power of People" as represented by governments and such world organisations as the United Nations, I want to return to *you* and ask, once again—"What do *you* think?"

Perhaps you will decide to reread this book to ponder some of the suggested ideas. Ask yourself questions about each chapter and try to see if any of the points raised can in any way be related to your own situation. What do *you* believe? What problems worry your faith? Do you have a simple trusting faith? Do you really know your objectives? Have you noticed some changes in your attitude towards life, and those around you, as various points have been brought to your notice? What kind of a person would you become if Love flowed into every situation? Are you prejudiced by habit and belief in other directions? If you are not tolerant to those around you, *why not?*

Honest questions illumine our minds with answers, and you can do much to clear your thinking by this method. The more you know about yourself, the more will you be able to create a firm foundation on which to build the castle of your dreams.

We can so easily miss the importance of searching questions in an extension of knowledge and in our relationships with family, friends, or job. And this personal analysis can extend through our habitual thinking processes right into the realms of inspiration and prayer.

Individuality is *not* self-contained. It is always a part of society. "No man is an island." By Divine plan, we evolve by mutual inter-dependence. The members of a family depend on each other's contributions to the well-being of all. The community, nations, and world family evolve, on all levels, through the service, thought, productivity, and work of everyone in them.

As individuals we are naturally deeply centred in self-awareness. Our own thoughts and experiences are intense and therefore we habitually project our personalities and ideas from the standpoint which we have accepted. We are just what we are by the accumulation of all we think and know.

One of the quickest ways to increase our knowledge and well-being is to turn our attention to the experience of others. The constant question, in every range of expression, to loved ones, friends, business associates and everyone we contact, could well be "What do *you* think?" or, "What do *you* know about this?" or, "In your experience, what did *you* do when faced with this problem?"

Such questions always bring answers. In any subject of which we have knowledge, we are only too happy to pass on what we know about it. And as we learn to ask and carefully listen it is astonishing how so many new factors and illuminating details emerge to extend our own concepts.

It is a truth that we learn best through other people and their contribution to knowledge and thought. No one is ever in a position where he cannot be helped forward by someone else. You, and I, always need the help and fellowship of others; even as they in turn need to receive what we have to offer.

When we begin to appreciate and practise spiritual principles and prayer, this is even more significant and applicable. Let us see why.

We live in the Spirit and Mind of God. And that same Life is in everyone else. We are individual parts of the Whole and, in this deeper sense, are always immersed in the Mind which initiates and sustains *every* life.

Perhaps we have a problem, or feel the need of some information, in order to achieve a specific objective. So we pray for inspiration and guidance. We have faith in the answer and sometimes wait endlessly for it to come into our minds.

In the meantime we are mixing with people and are involved in conversation about many things. How often, to the listening ear, the answer to our prayer is to be found in this exchange. But how often do we fail to recognise it when it appears!

The Father ever seeks to create this fellowship, this union of people through love, and correspondingly is constantly sharing His inspiration, help, guidance and power in this way.

You will be following the paths of wisdom and spiritual truth if you listen to other people's ideas as well as expressing your own. You will uncover Divine Wisdom as you ask questions about your thoughts, problems and projects, and listen to the responses you receive.

Pray, but let your prayers bring you into close communion with others, for God may well speak to you through them, or even through the lips of a child.

Having said this, let us pass on to the concept of abiding in the Presence, ever open and receptive to His word, inspiration, peace, love and perfect everything. It brings us to that centre of stillness in which the Spirit dwells. "Be still . . . and know that I am God."

In our final discussion we will behold the great vision of our inheritance as people—just people in this God-created world.

POWER THOUGHTS

1 Questions—whether asked of God or people—provoke a reply for your appreciation and assessment.
2 Be ready each day to ask God questions about anything. But always be attentive and receptive to the answers. Sometimes the answer will come inspirationally: other times through people.
3 Get to know your neighbour by inquiring about his problems and life. Let him glimpse God through you.
4 Your mind will glow with new interest and knowledge as your relationship with your neighbour strengthens day by day. Your new interest will soon be reciprocated to the benefit of all.

TALKING TO GOD

And call upon me in the day of trouble; I will deliver thee, and thou shalt glorify me.—PSALM 50: 15.

I like to talk to God because He heeds the words I say.
For when I speak to humankind their thoughts drift far away;
At times they scarce reply to me, and often from their tone
I know their minds are busy with some tangle of their own.
But God will lean from Heaven be it morning, noon or night,
To take my troubles in His hands and gently set them right.

I like to talk to God because He ever seems to care
And as I pour my problems out I feel my Father's there.
It's not that way with other men, they seldom want to know
The story of my blunders, or my heartaches, or my woe.
But God stands close beside me and He whispers to me, "Son,
Let's scan your worries over and I'll solve them, one by one."

I like to talk to God because He likes to talk to me,
He loves to share my burdens when I bring them to His knee.
E'en folk I call my dearest friends grow tired of my affairs,
Before I've even ended they begin to tell me theirs!
But HE is ever mindful of each small perplexity.
It's good to talk to God because HE ALWAYS ANSWERS ME.

"MAC"

Chapter 14

THE INFINITE POWER OF PEOPLE

I STOOD IN the United Nations Plaza in New York and contemplated the international scene in which delegates from 117 nations congregate to seek, by consultation and negotiation, to solve the problems of war and the needs of mankind. Etched, simply, on a white wall I found this idealistic statement: "They shall beat their swords into plowshares and their spears into pruning hooks. Nation shall not lift up sword against nation, neither shall they learn war any more."

Across the lawns, overlooking the Hudson River, the vast Assembly Hall nestles at the base of the rectangular block of skyscraper offices of the United Nations. And, on tall poles in the foreground, the flags of 117 member countries flutter in the breeze, their exotic colours blending like a mass of flowers in an old-world garden.

The flow of delegates, visitors and tourists fills the square with life—a coming and going through the main entrance resembling busy ants entering their nest. And here, as people pass by, can be heard the languages of the world.

I sat in one of the Council Chambers and listened to the delegates of the assembled nations discussing their problems in the field of human rights. The circular dais, with sections allotted to each nation's representatives, seemed to centre the great stillness which pervaded this magnificent auditorium. Only the voice of the speaking delegate could be heard, sometimes in a foreign language which was simultaneously translated into English and relayed to the earphones I was wearing.

Contemplating this inspiring scene I pondered and prayed and, in the Great Silence, there came a quickening assurance that the true destiny of man was secure, and that it would unfold, step by step, as human needs and rights forced the pace and led the nations to consult and work together as a family under God.

Behind each delegate was the government he represented. But behind each government I became intensely aware of the teeming millions of simple family men and women who yearned for peace, freedom, food, shelter and progressive prosperity.

There is a deep, permanent and hungry ideal which slumbers in the heart of every man of every race, colour or creed. It is forever struggling for expression even though sometimes it becomes submerged in war, lost in social malpractices, and twisted by injustice, disease, poverty or greed.

The fires of evolution have scorched our generation in many ways, but the very pains have turned our thoughts to the humanitarian need to work together as a world family of nations. Yet this high ideal can be achieved only through trial and error, failure and success.

There is often a feeling of disillusionment as the peoples of the world remember the collapse of the first ideals of the League of Nations, and see the political manœuvring and conflicts which have so often betrayed the lofty purposes of the United Nations. But these are the growing pains of the new order. The very pressure of events increasingly awakens the knowledge that all our major problems, personal, national and international, are essentially spiritual problems which ultimately can be solved only by an all-out implementation of spiritual principles.

In the meantime there is an urgent need for everyone in the world to recognise, accept and undergird in faith and prayer all the works of the United Nations. We must stand fast, with single-minded purpose, to the ideal of a united world and know that in the end it will be the focal point of spiritual integrity and expression.

It is equally urgent that we should all look beyond every appearance of failure, beholding only the perfect vision of the objectives of the United Nations Organisation, and appreciate the immense works that are being done through its many agencies and activities.

The United Nations is operative in every major field of national and international well-being—atomic energy, labour, education, science, culture, reconstruction and development, monetary funds, civil aviation, communications, meteorological research, tariffs, trade, children's fund, and the like.

I sat listening to the speakers and abiding in God's Presence. What would the Father want in these various affairs of man? I think we all know the answer. It came to me that we should all pray daily with love and faith that every delegate, and everyone who serves in any capacity in the United Nations, shall be filled night and day with the Holy Spirit.

When a multitude is united in positive faith, love and prayer, then the signs and wonders of God follow. Every day pray—"Thank You, Father. Thy Spirit fills every heart and mind throughout the United Nations. Thy Love, Wisdom and Guidance are freely manifesting in all concerned."

Great and sometimes grave responsibilities rest on these delegates. They, too, become weary and careworn. Let us undergird them with love and prayer so that they may ever be lifted up to hear the clear call of mankind which is directed to them, and receive God's strength in every need.

*   *   *

To show that others are not unaware of the responsibility and spiritual challenge, I now intend to quote some illuminating extracts from broadcasts given by a number of leading personalities who were asked to speak on the "Minute for Peace" religious radio programme. Who better to start with than the Secretary General U Thant who said:

"We live in a world of noise, yet our conscience is called the still, small voice. As Dag Hammarskjold once pointed out, 'We all have within us a centre of stillness surrounded by silence.' Unless we heed our own conscience, we shall continue to be attracted by what is loud and garish, and lose our sense of values. If there is no peace in the world today, it is because there is no peace in the minds of men.

"It is important, therefore, that all of us should determine to set aside some time each day to commune with ourselves, to talk with our own still, small voices, to devote even one minute for thoughts of peace and goodwill.

"The General Assembly of the United Nations begins and ends every session with one minute of silent prayer. That is a good example for all of us to follow in our daily lives."

Dr. G. P. Malalasekera, High Commissioner of Ceylon to the United Kingdom, broadcast:

" 'Hatred does not cease by hatred. Hatred ceases only by love.' So declared the Buddha, 2,500 years ago. Till human hearts are filled with thoughts of love and compassion there will be no real peace in the world. The mind has within it forces greater than the atom. If, at a given moment each day, a thousand million minds would be simultaneously concentrated on a single thought—the thought of goodwill and peace—the power so generated could irresistibly move the leaders of men and those whom they lead. Conflicts and tensions will then disappear and Peace will reign over the earth."

Lord Caradon, permanent representative of the United Kingdom to the United Nations, stated:

"Those of us who work in and for the United Nations realise that there is now a new factor in the world. Now, whenever there is a dispute, there is a small team of men led by the Secretary General of the United Nations who bring to the dispute not the old tests of national advantage or national greed or national pride, but the new tests of international advantage and the benefit of the ordinary people concerned. That is the new thing in the world."

Here are the words of Dr. Francisco Quevas Cancino, the Ambassador of Mexico to the United Nations:

"Beyond the beating of modern life the Spirit of every human being remains intact. It is always there, always conscious of its own being, always certain of the road to virtue, but rather than meditating and listening to it, we prefer to be stunned by the myths of progress. Our salvation rests on the contrary in listening to the voice of our other self, in following its directives and not ours, in listening to its words and not the ones of our passion. What man can be saved from the whirl of today without listening for a moment to the voice of tomorrow?"

His Holiness, Pope Paul VI, proclaimed:

"First of all, as peacemakers, we must love peace, we must meditate and reveal immediate peace. We must conform our minds to the thought of peace. We must love peace, because its dwelling is first in men's hearts. Peace must live and lie in men's consciences. With this order in relation to all, and in the relation to men, it is wisdom, it is justice, it is civilisation. Whoever loves peace, loves mankind without distinctions of race or colour."

The President of the 19th Session of the United Nations General Assembly, H. E. Alex Quasson-Sackey, Foreign Minister of Ghana, broadcast this message:

"We are living in a very uneasy world today. Desire for peace is not enough. We must work hard to remove the root causes which create friction between nation and nation, and between man and man. We should accept man as man, and let our endeavours centre around promoting good and happy relations between human beings. We should devote a minute each day to silence in which to examine ourselves and find out if in our individual lives we accept every man whether he be yellow, white or black as part of the human race. It is only when there is a moral conscience that man is not an end, but a means to an end, that we can hope to achieve an effective peace."

The United Nations Information Officer for International Co-operation Year, Nazsi Rashel, said:

"At this time when the world is struggling to solve its problems through international co-operation, I bring you the quiet voice and words of Mahatma Gandhi:

" 'There is an indefinable mysterious power that pervades everything. I feel it, though I do not see it. It is this unseen power which makes itself felt and yet defies all proof, because it is so unlike all that I perceive through my senses. I do dimly perceive that whilst everything around me is ever changing, ever dying, there is underlying all that change, a living power that is changeless, that holds all together.' "

Here also are wise words by three Presidents of the United States:

"And more than ever we support the United Nations, as the best instrument yet devised to promote the peace of the world and to promote the well-being of mankind." —Lyndon B. Johnson.

"All Americans should get to know about the United Nations and prepare themselves and their children for the task of sustaining it."—Dwight D. Eisenhower.

"In the development of the United Nations lies the only true alternative to war . . . mankind must put an end to war, or war will put an end to mankind."—John F. Kennedy.

*   *   *

I was invited to speak in the United Nations Chapel under the auspices of this "Minute for Peace" prayer project. So humbly and thankfully aware of the common bond and heritage of all mankind, and quickened with respect for the high ideal and purpose of the United Nations, may I share with you what I was inspired to say?

"We are here in the United Nations Chapel, right alongside the United Nations building in New York. This beautiful edifice rises to the sky, to house the representatives of 117 nations of earth. The flags of all these nations bravely fly all round the entrance to symbolise the ideal of unity.

"The astonishing truth is that we are right now in the very centre of a world activity which daily shapes the destiny of all mankind. What a privilege and honour it is for the people of the United States that the United Nations has its home and headquarters in New York.

"Even as I speak many of the greatest minds, representing a multitude of other great minds, in all the countries of earth, are seeking to find the way whereby man can live safely upon the world. They examine not only the political problems and needs of each nation in relationship to every other nation, but undertake a massive work in helping to advance the well-being of underdeveloped nations. Their vision and activity in famine areas, food production, illiteracy, education, technical aid, finance, science, communications and special help in every national and international need, are wondrous new factors in world evolution. Never in the history of mankind has so vast a project ever reached anything approaching the vision, effectiveness and maturity now manifesting in the United Nations.

"Although one sees many difficulties, although one would wish for the total idealism on which it is founded coming into total expression, I would remind you that for every failure, there have been many resounding successes. A tremendous work is going on through the co-operative efforts of the nations of the world seeking to solve major problems.

"There is still a lot to do, of course, but what a wonderful age in which it can be done! What a wonderful vision mankind has today! It works for peace. It knows that peace is not a static state of non-activity. We have to work for it and earn it in love and justice for all. It challenges and invites the highest idealism, integrity and determination of everyone everywhere. It represents the deepest spiritual yearning and vision inherent in every soul on earth!

"One of the most heartening factors across the world today is the increasing recognition that it is in the acceptance and activation of spiritual principles that we really find our common heritage. It is in these spiritual principles that we discover the answers to all human problems. It is in the spiritual vision of all religions too that, strangely enough, after much conflict in the ages gone by, we are finding a common bond. Confronted by the dangerous problems which mankind has to deal with today, this common bond, of a common God, is found to be the common good inherent in every religion based upon love, worship, brotherhood, prayer, faith and a belief in the destiny of mankind.

"So it is a moment for them, for you, or anyone who hears these words to lift your vision, that you might be that light which shines in the darkness, that you might be the channel undergirding the entire concept of all the nations of earth. While we are accustomed to government decisions and to the decisions of the United Nations, on political levels, we are not yet very accustomed to the idea that the entire fabric of every nation is the *you* and the *me*, the individuals without whom there could be no nations at all. That is why I am very conscious of the fact that man only speaks and activates Truth when he speaks and works with the well-being of all mankind in mind.

"I speak as a man of the people. I speak for the African, the people of India, and the Middle East. I speak for the

Chinese, yearning and searching to find a foothold in the affairs of man. I speak for the Russian people. I speak for those who are hungry and weak and old and heavy laden. I speak for the sick of the world. I speak for those who have very little of this world's goods. I speak for the millionaires, and for all the children. I speak for the family men and women of earth.

"I meet these people around the world, and they all want peace. They yearn, as families, to be able to live satisfactorily, to look after their children, to provide ways and means whereby they might advance. All I have ever discovered about people has been the pulsing, sensitive heart of love that only needs breathing room in order to live. Family men and women never want war, and everyone everywhere loathes anything that has to do with slaughter, or the burning of cities and villages, or anything that violates the sanctity of the human family.

"Therefore my plea to you, my plea to the United Nations, my plea to Governments in the name of all that is sacred in the mind of God, is that we shall return to an absolute reverence for life; the kind of reverence Albert Schweitzer decreed; the reverence all great thinkers know to be true; the reverence all spiritual leaders the world over proclaim. The most practical and most urgent challenge facing mankind is a total allegiance to this LOVE, this reverence, which is the central teaching of Jesus Christ, Buddha, the Prophets, Mahatma Gandhi, the leaders of every Church and religion, the Pope, saints and mystics, and the instinctive yearning of all people everywhere. We fulfil God's laws or perish from the earth.

"I pray therefore that we may each accept our personal

responsibility for the establishment of peace in our own lives and, therefore, in the world. Even one person, abiding in the stillness of God with simple faith and love, brings Divine illumination to all mankind. In love and prayer we can undergird the work of the United Nations and know that the Father is inspiring and guiding them all.

"Minutes for peace each day mean time spent with God, believing that the illimitable movement of the Holy Spirit is producing multiplying good in all the affairs of man the world over.

"Thank You, Father. And may Thy Will be done in the establishment of the Brotherhood of Man, in the Fatherhood of God, on earth as it is in heaven."

*   *   *

I am sure life should be constantly balanced by love and laughter, recreation and simple pleasures. If we get too serious—then we ARE too serious, and we become caught in a rigidity of mind and outlook which restrict relaxation and creative impulses. In spiritual searching, too, we can so easily become so seriously intent upon our project that we lose sight of the fact that true spiritual expression brings us into warm, happy and tolerant relationships. If we are too complicated—we are indeed too complicated, and need to rediscover simple ways.

People are people, all seeking the best possible expression according to their awakening ability to understand and achieve it. As one travels widely the differences of race, colour, customs and ideology dissolve in the common humanity which forever blends with our own needs and aspirations.

Late one night, while on a mission in the United Church of South India as guest of the Bishop of Coimbatore, I wandered the city streets. Unashamedly I cried in the darkness as I contemplated hundreds of men, women and children, huddled sleeping like bundles of rags on the dusty pavements. No homes, little food and, perhaps, little hope.

The hungry cry of India, the "winds of change" in Africa, the blood and sweat, pain and tears of Vietnam and the Berlin Wall, all scream in our conscience, and will, eventually, prise wide open the doors of our infinite wells of compassion. This is the true vision and leadership inspiring the works of the United Nations, the churches, and all people of goodwill in their own responsible personal dedication and contribution.

Just people—everywhere, east or west, north or south. I am now remembering my last visit to the beautiful tropical island of Ceylon and its warm-hearted people. What a spontaneous welcome I received from a host of friends so easily made on a visit four years previously. How great is the reward of friendship not forgotten, but found again in reunion!

In the days of services in the Colombo Christian Churches, I found only love and the longing of people to be established in growing faith and spiritual understanding. Even in the midst of a community which is ninety per cent Buddhist, and the minority Christians and Hindus, there is this yearning, as everywhere else, to live together as a family entity with well-being for all. Here, as elsewhere, there are the interminable conflicts of opinion, methods and means, but all pointing to the path of sublimation and progression.

It is always a Divine Finger pointing to the truth when,

as I found, Christians, Buddhists and Hindus came to our Christian services and followed the way of Love.

I travelled on an overnight train up into the mountains to Bandarawella. The dawn spread its glory over the beautiful tea estates on the hills, and the shadows swept away from the nestling villages in the valleys. The cool highland air after the heat of Colombo was a benediction indeed to an Englishman fresh from the rain, frost and fog of winter in the British Isles.

Warm hospitality to the stranger is endemic in Ceylon—with plenty of curry to make it warmer! After early morning service I wandered happily with the minister down the crowded and twisting main street of Bandarawella.

In many eastern cities and towns the European is captivated by the colourful scene of men in strange head-dresses and skirt-like sarongs, and the women dressed in brilliant saris, with jet black hair and a glint of earrings and bangles. Above all, he notices the happy ease with which they mix and chatter.

Shopping provides the opportunity to gossip and laugh together. The shops are all open to the street and huddled side by side. In a seemingly endless procession on the pavement, copper-coloured vendors proclaim the merits of piles of oranges, coconuts, vegetables and all manner of exotic fruits. A tailor at his sewing machine; the umbrella repairer with a pile of broken ones beside him; the betelnut merchant; a huge stack of woven wicker baskets; jewellers making brooches and bracelets; a slab with cut fillets of fish and a cloud of flies! The butcher and a mound of dubious-looking cuts; a chorus of cackles from boxes full of hens for sale; pots and pans and kerosene stoves; a display of sticky looking cakes, and a thousand other marketable wares.

Oxen pull covered carts full of new merchandise; a battered car or two crazily sweep a honking pathway through the scattering people; brown-skinned, laughing children scamper in play. An old bus, overcrowded with people, sets off with a rattle and a roar towards homes up the valley. The people shop and talk and are content.

Naturally, like any other tourist, I wanted to take as many photographs as possible. I began tentatively and a little surreptitiously to snap the shoppers and the owners of produce in their open stalls. In a few minutes it seemed as though all the people in this street scene were eagerly helping me to do so. They laughed and chattered, and presented me with a host of interesting characters and opportunities. Ladies in saris, long-bearded men, labourers carrying sacks of flour; the butcher, the baker, the candlestick maker—the lot!

And, in an inner and wonderful way, I felt the simplicity of a natural fellowship with people who had spontaneously become friends. In one shop I was given a cool drink, and everywhere I felt like a boy, full of joy and laughter and peace, let loose to play. Just people—together.

I travelled on the morning train to Kandy, the ancient capital of Celonese kings. For four hours we wound round the sides of the glorious mountains, with their miles of tea plantations. Deep valleys, rivers, sunshine, and the cumulus clouds building fairy cities against the blue sky. Down and down, from six thousand feet to about fifteen hundred feet at Kandy.

A crowded service here in the great Anglican church near the famous Buddhist Temple of the Tooth, reputed to contain a tooth of Buddha. Exotic gardens, palms, the sacred lake, a thronging town. Then, next morning, on by car to Kurunegala.

It was such a beautiful drive through the coconut groves, rubber plantations and exuberant green country-side. Bullock carts; a crowd of happy children playing in a muddy stream; a water buffalo lying in the water; an elephant pulling a roller to level the road; villages, always crowded with happy people, and the open shops; a Buddhist monk in saffron robes, walking shaded from the hot sunshine by a huge red umbrella. Then the hustling, hot town of Kurunegala. Cool drinks, lunch and a siesta in the home of a good friend in his coconut grove.

In the late afternoon, an hour or so before the service in the Anglican church, a Hindu gentleman, his wife and other members of his family arrived. They had come to pay their respects to me, and to express their thanks for the wonderful healing the husband had received on my last visit some four years previously. And, as he talked, my thoughts swept back in vivid memory to the occasion.

As now, I had then been preparing to leave the home of my host for a meeting when a messenger came from a bungalow down the road to ask if the Christian man of prayer would come to intercede for the head of the household who was unconscious and dying. I went with him.

On the verandah of this home the large family and relatives had assembled to pay their last respects. I was ushered into an inner room, and there on a single bed the sick man lay, unconscious and breathing laboriously.

Some of the family crept quietly into the room and others stood in the doorway. I knelt at the side of the bed and was about to pray in words when a wondrous stillness filled the room and I could not speak.

We were held, poised, in the quietness and could only recognise the Presence of God. In a few minutes the man's breathing became quiet. He opened his eyes, smiled, looked round. Still no words—until, finally, I whispered, "Thank You, Father," rose, and quietly went away.

The man was healed in that hour. Next day he was up and soon back to work. I heard this good news before I left Ceylon.

And now, four years later, here was this Hindu gentleman, strong and healthy, visiting me to tell of the Blessed event in his life when, as a Christian united with Hindus, we prayed together for him. Thank God!

The population of Ceylon, for centuries, has been depleted by widespread malarial infection. Then the World Health Organisation, an agency of the United Nations, introduced comprehensive work to clear the causes and stop the disease. Today, malaria has virtually been eliminated from this island.

These are the new works of a new age and, in ultimate outreach, lead to the fulfilment of the innermost needs and hopes of mankind for peace, health, happiness and abundant life.

*　　*　　*

Just people! The wide world over! And that is why we must always begin with ourselves and our own responsibility and personal contribution to the well-being of everyone else. For they, like us, are . . . just people!

POWER THOUGHTS

1 The Power-thinking, God-centred personality recognises at once the equality of all people of every race, colour and creed.

2 In the end only people matter so what happens to mankind will be the full expression of the mental-spiritual outcome and thought of the world community.

3 As an individual you are important to God, the Creator, and therefore have the great responsibility of implementing His Divine Plan where you are, today and tomorrow.

4 I see you now poised and centred in God. Through Him you radiate Love, Faith and Purpose so that you may bring peace to yourself and those around you. You are a blessing to all whose lives touch yours.

*   *   *

As we come to the close of my book I can see you going forward to a new and rich life. The spirit of the Lord is always with you for He has prepared the perfect way for you to tread the rest of your days.

As a person of love, faith and prayer, you are indeed a Power Thinker, always reflecting the thoughts of God in every experience. In Him, you are the Light of the world. And thank You, Father, that it is so.

AFFIRMATION

God is a Spirit; and they that worship him must worship him in spirit and in truth.—JOHN 4: 24.

> *Come, let me drink of Truth's eternal well,*
> *Pure and pellucid and ineffable.*
> *I am a Spirit, of the Father made;*

Radiant, invincible and unafraid.
The life of God throughout my being thrills,
Immutable as the immortal hills.

There is no end in Spirit; from this plane
I soar but to renew my life again.
There are no bonds in Spirit; I am free
As winds of heaven and the trackless sea.
Claiming the Spark Divine that gave me birth,
I travel changeless o'er a changing earth.

God is in everything I sense or see . . .
God in the Universe and GOD IN ME.

"MAC"